WOUNDED

WOUNDED

Vietnam to Iraq

Ronald J. Glasser, M.D.

GEORGE BRAZILLER / NEW YORK

First published in 2006 by George Braziller, Inc.

For information, please address the publisher:

George Braziller, Inc.
171 Madison Avenue
New York, NY 10016
www.georgebraziller.com
Telephone: 212.889.0909
Fax: 212.689.5405

Library of Congress Cataloging-in-Publication Data

Glasser, Ronald J.
Wounded : Vietnam to Iraq / Ronald J. Glasser
          p. cm.
ISBN-13: 978-0-8076-1571-3 (hardback)
ISBN-13: 978-0-8076-1569-0 (pbk.)
1. Soldiers—Wounds and injuries—United States. 2.
Soldiers—Health and hygiene—United States. 3. Soldiers—Mental health—
United States. 4. United States—Armed Forces—Medical care.
5. Vietnamese Conflict, 1961-1975—Health aspects. 6. Iraq War,
2003—Health aspects. I. Title.
UH223.G637 2006
355.3'45097309045—dc22
2006008173

A portion of this book appeared in different form in *Harper's*.
Printed and bound in the United States of America
Designed by Rita Lascaro

CONTENTS

DEDICATION

In respect and admiration for General Hal Moore, arguably the boldest and finest battalion commander to serve in Vietnam; Joe Galloway, the only reporter during three wars to be awarded the U.S. Army's Bronze Star with "V," signifying extraordinary valor, for saving, at great risk to himself, the lives of wounded troopers during the four-day battle of the Ia Drang Valley, November 1965; and H. R. McMaster, West Point graduate, at this moment commanding the Third Armored Cavalry Regiment somewhere in Iraq along the Syrian border. . .

FOREWORD

These stories are true. I was part of some of them; the rest belonged to others. What was so troubling was not what I saw or heard, but that it all kept happening again and again.

In fairness, it has been a brutal and frightening time for those who bear the burden of this war, while those who speak the truth are officially censured or personally attacked. So in some cases, I've changed the names, dates, deployments, and unit designations, as well as the sequence of events. The technical data, the medicine, the weapon systems, the successful tactics and unsuccessful strategies, all that is available to anyone who is willing to look.

As for me, none of this was written out of pique or anger, but to give those caught up in this terrible enterprise something all their own, something they could give to others and say, "This is what happened."

If there is something more to be said, it will have to be said by others, although I wonder how they will do it. I doubt that there is a novel in any of this and the politics can become quite tedious and heavy-handed. The wounds, of course, the penetrating head injuries, the mangled legs and lost arms, the closed head trauma, the grief and depression, the blindness and the pain, all speak for themselves. For the dead we still have our poets: "You think their dying is the worst thing that could happen. Then they stay dead."

WOUNDED

All the Pauls

So this is how it happens. And it happens all the time. A bright eighteen-year-old kid decides that college is not for him. He asks around and somehow finds out that the Marines have a deferred enlistment program available at the beginning of the senior year in high school that allows recruits their choice of any three Military Occupational Specialties: artillery, tanks, or low level antiaircraft. Always interested in cars and trucks, and realizing the advantage of choosing the type of duty that he wants or at least fancies, the eighteen-year-old chooses to be a tanker and decides to enlist at the beginning of his senior year. Whatever else may happen, at least he will not have to walk into battle.

The parents, not pleased with the decision, take their

son aside and caution him that this should not be a frivolous or casual choice, that there are real, grown-up consequences to deciding to go into the military, including being killed, getting wounded, or even being taken prisoner with the risk of torture. But "Paul" will have none of it, insisting that he will be careful; and so, unable to either stop or dissuade him, a month after high school graduation he is in the Marines. Two weeks later, after saying good-bye to his friends, he is on his way to San Diego for thirteen weeks of basic training. He is strangely pleased and oddly comforted that basic training in the Marines is the longest and most demanding of all the armed forces. Paul might be young, but he is no fool. He understands that if you want to be the best, you have to be taught how to be the best, and that always takes time—lots of time.

Paul never wavered or faltered. With a growing maturity, he accepted the rigors and even the foolishness of basic training as a method as well as a system, sure that, even if not quite comprehensible to those going through it all, the training had real value in the long term and was best tolerated and even embraced, if not so much to get along, as to gain something useful and maybe even of permanent value.

After basic training, he went to four weeks of MCT, Marine Combat Training. In the Army, it is called Advanced Infantry Training, but for the Marines, it is simply something everyone does. MCT was a month of weapons firing and weapons management. He learned how to use all the individual and crew-served weapons in the Marine arsenal. There was little joking around and less humor. Weapons were a serious business. Everyone understood that this was no longer merely training, but life and death.

Following MCT, Paul went on to two and a half months of tank school at Fort Knox, where he learned machinery, maintenance, and some gunnery. Most of the month was straight classroom work with less than a week in the field. But on the second day out on the tank course, he knew he'd made the right choice.

The M1A1 battle tank had a 120-millimeter smoothbore cannon. The British Challenger 2 Main Battle Tank had a 120-millimeter rifled barrel. But the rounds from the M1A1 had a higher muzzle velocity than the 120 rifled cannon, leaving the gun at more than 3200 feet per second. And the M1A1 weighed seventy tons and, with its gas turbine engine, could go through or over anything at fifty miles an hour. Whatever else anyone might think of armor, he'd be the biggest kid on the block.

There was more training, more honing of skills, more understanding of what it was to be a Marine and then what it was to be a Marine at war. Paul liked it all. He liked the camaraderie. He liked the effort and being in something bigger than himself. He liked the sense of commitment and duty, of responsibility and honor. He even liked the crusty old sergeants who never married because the Marine Corps had never issued them a wife.

Following tank school, Paul became a member of Alpha Company, First Tank Battalion, First Marine Division. Two years after the fall of Baghdad in April 2003, with Alpha Company, First Battalion, he arrived in Iraq to become part of a regimental combat team designated RCT 2.

Unlike conventional formations where armor is massed to attack other armored units or held in reserve to crush pockets of resistance, the Marines, despite the pronouncements coming out of Washington that the war had been won, understood that the war had simply changed, demanding different tactics and a different military structure. They gave up the large units that had raced to Baghdad in 2003 and reorganized their force structure to meet the new challenge.

The Marine command distributed their tanks out among the combat platoons, putting the tanks up front with the troops on the ground, rumbling through the streets of Iraq's towns and villages, inching forward side by side with grunts as they put up roadblocks and swept through towns and villages, supplying both offensive power and, when necessary, immediate backup.

A regimental combat team is a powerful, focused military unit combining ground troops, tanks, cobra gun ships, and when possible air support. The Marine doctrine is not so much "quicker, faster, more agile" as it is to "hurt 'em and kill 'em." RCTs are not nation builders nor are they promoters of democracy. They break things.

The tactics and rules of engagement are simple. Ground units move forward with their tanks for cover. The tanks, with their enormous weight and firepower, keep pace with the grunts. It is an intimate and immediate kind of warfare, with little room for error and none for a mistake.

That is what happened during Operation Matador, an attempt to make up for the earlier mistakes to suppress insurgent activity and clear the bad guys out of the towns and villages surrounding the Sunni Triangle. This time they would do it right—no hesitation, no compromise. Paul's tank moved down a side street with a squad of Marines going house to house to check for weapons and insurgents. A quarter of the way through one of the dozens of towns, a number of grunts entering a house came under fire.

The Marines had entered the house where insurgents were hiding in the basement. Shooting up through the floorboards, a half-dozen Marines were killed and wounded within minutes of their entering the house.

The rules of engagement had been quite clear: any tank rounds were to be used sparingly with every effort to limit collateral damage. As soon as the Marines exited the house carrying the dead and wounded, Paul's tank put three rounds into the building, with rocks and debris and shrapnel careening through the neighborhood. The rounds killed everyone inside the building. After a few minutes, the tanks and the grunts moved on. Leveling the building probably saved a lot of Marines coming up behind them, but it didn't win them any friends on that street.

A week later, the insurgents changed their tactics. They started placing the explosives in the center of the road and pressure plates as detonators along the curbs. The roadside bombs had been just that, road-side bombs; when they were detonated they might blow a track off a tank or destroy one of the wheel mounts, but little else. But these bombs exploded under the vehicles. The weight of the tanks set off the pressure plates. The first time it happened, the force of the blast was so great that it warped the six-inch steel plates along the bottom of the tank. The blast killed or wounded everyone inside.

There isn't all that much a nineteen-year-old can say about dying. Few in an RCT think of death. They might think about getting wounded, but not being killed. When you are young and in the Marines, death is for someone else. But his friends had been there in the morning and gone that night. Paul missed them and was terribly troubled, as he helped the captain box up their gear and belongings, that he knew something, something important, that none of their families knew, that no one who had cared for them or loved them or waited for them, knew or could even have guessed. And that seemed wrong. The real meaning of those deaths and of loss would come later.

There was a kind of grimness that settled in after the bombings. The sweeps continued and more Marines were killed and even more wounded; but so were a lot of Iraqis. Bad guys and good guys were killed. And sometimes, in trying to kill Americans, they killed their own. There were days, moving on from dawn to dusk, where one town and village merged into the next and when out of nowhere and quite unexpectedly a bomb would go off and they would go on to level a street or maybe a whole neighborhood. They slept next to their tanks and didn't shower for weeks. There were days when supplies could not get through and they had to cut to half rations. They worried about having enough gas just to keep going.

There were rumors that insurgents had begun to hang their IEDs, improvised explosive devices, from the overhead lampposts that lined the areas' major boulevards. When they blew, the explosion and shrapnel rained down instead of up, killing or wounding everyone riding on top of the armored vehicles. Paul heard they literally blew off the heads of drivers using the opened forward hatches of the armored personal carriers to steer their APCs. He didn't know if any of it was true, but it could have been.

But what he was sure about was what happened one evening at one of their checkpoints. A car, turning a corner, didn't stop. It was dusk and difficult to see, but the car simply kept moving. A car bomb could kill anyone within fifty-five meters. There was never a lot of time at checkpoints, and when the car, ignoring the hand signals, seemed to speed up, the Humvee blocking the intersection opened fire. The 50-caliber machine gun tore the Toyota apart. Inside, they found a family, a mother and three girls, killed, the fully jacketed high-velocity rounds having blown them apart. None of them knew what to do. So they left the car where it was and simply moved on.

All the letters home, all the e-mails and even the calls were the same. Despite the increasing numbers of casualties and deepening sense of disorder, if not confusion, everyone said things were fine and they were OK, and that if not winning, they weren't losing. But mostly they told their families not to worry. Paul made sure when there was time that he wrote or sent an e-mail home every day. For the most part, he wrote about the other guys in the unit, how they were all doing what they'd trained to do, how they made sure they took care of each other as well as taking care of themselves. That seemed enough. You don't lie in the Marines. But that doesn't mean you have to tell the whole truth.

They pushed their tanks well past maintenance guidelines. They had no choice. There were no tanks in reserve, and with replacement parts at a premium, they just kept moving. But the constant wear, as well as the sand and dirt that got into everything, began to cause breakdowns. The heat only made it all worse. By midday you could fry an egg on the tank's armor plate. After three weeks of unending alerts and constant fighting, the hubs on the drive wheels and the main bolts holding the wheels to the treads locked up.

Late one morning, they finally had to pull over and work on the gear train. Exhausted, having pushed on for days, Paul and the gunner, tired and grim, took the main spanner out of the toolbox and, climbing out of the tank, started to work on the hubs. A couple of grunts set up a mini-roadblock at the nearest intersection to give them some cover. Pressing down on the back of the spanner for leverage, the head of the spanner slipped off the hub, shearing off the neck of the bolt. There was a moment when the pain left him stunned. A spasm of nausea swept over him as he grabbed his face and fell to the ground.

Even weeks later, it would be impossible to know exactly what happened. It could have been anything—a heat-expanded hub, an overworked bearing, not wearing the prescribed eye protection, too much force on the spanner, a weakened piece of metal from weeks of taking sniper rounds, or even some shrapnel from IEDs or mortars denting the rotor mounts—but a piece of metal had torn into his left eye.

A Humvee took him to an FST, a Forward Surgical Team, set up about a kilometer outside the town they had just quaranteed and begun to sweep. The surgeon examined the eye and putting on a simple bandage, called in a chopper that took him to the Twenty-fourth Surgical Hospital at Balad, forty miles north-northwest of Baghdad. An hour later, his eye was patched and he was being flown to Landstuhl Regional Medical Center in Germany. At Landstuhl, they sewed up the major laceration of his eye and within half a dozen hours he was on a C-130 medevac to Bethesda Naval Hospital in Bethesda, Maryland.

A CAT scan in Germany had shown metal fragments embedded in the globe of Paul's eye close to the retina, as well as in the tissues at the very back of the socket near the optic nerve. Whatever had happened, the damage was clearly the result of a low-velocity impact. It hadn't been lost on him, listening to the doctors talk among themselves, that had it been a splinter from a round ricocheting off the side of the tank or a piece of shrapnel from a mortar or a roadside bomb, the metal fragments would have surely penetrated his skull and entered the frontal lobes of his brain.

There was some initial hope that the retina had remained intact and that the globe of the eye that had filled with blood would eventually clear so that some sight would return to the damaged eye. Still, there were problems outside of the traumatic injury itself. One of the problems was infection; another was getting out the fragments without making things worse. A CAT scan only gives a two-dimensional image; so the surgeons working within a very small space would have a difficult time finding the fragments in what in reality is a three-dimensional field. And simply exploring the eye might just stir things up, increasing the pressures within the globe, damaging the eye even more.

But to leave the metal in place might lead to an allergic reaction, a kind of massive response from the body's immune system to the foreign objects, as well as to the already damaged parts of the eye itself, resulting in the immune system not only attacking and destroying the tissues of the bad eye, but of the good eye as well, leading to the possibility of total blindness.

The surgeons decided to wait, to give the damaged eye a chance to calm down and to allow time for some of the blood to clear in order to give them better access to the intraocular fragments, all the while watching for any signs of infection in the damaged eye along with rejection in the good eye.

Paul was told the risks and the benefits of waiting. There would be a better chance of removing the metal fragments if they waited, but by waiting he might lose the vision in his right eye. There are no easy or simple decisions in a war. Once committed to the battlefield, the world is no longer the same. Old customs lose importance and familiar rituals their power. No second opinions here, no informed consent forms, no search of the Internet, no discussion of best practice guidelines. At age nineteen or thirty-five, a Marine decides for himself.

Paul took a deep breath and decided to wait. It would be a race; but his life had become a kind of race. When he finally did call home, it was only to tell his parents that he had been wounded, but that he was fine, that he was healing and the doctors were confident that he would be all right. And he meant it. He understood that whatever might happen, he'd survive. No small thing . . .

Four weeks later, the vision in his left eye had returned to 20/80. He could see—not well—but he could see. His good eye had remained normal, but he was having headaches because of the blurred vision on the left. The plan was to wait another two or three weeks and then go in after the metal fragments.

But over those weeks the vision in his damaged eye had dimmed a bit more and there was some growing concern that the nerves might have been damaged—so it is all still up in the air—as to how it will end.

What is clear though, and will never change, is that like so many others, despite resolve and determination, his life will never be the same. At best, there will always be that blurring to whatever he sees. In any war, but particularly this one, you can run, but you can't hide . . .

Realities

Medics

*"If there is a disaster, who are you going to ask about it?
Someone sitting on their ass, making self-serving pronouncements a couple of thousand miles away, or someone
in the middle of all the shit?"*

— CONVERSATION: WOUNDED MEDIC, SURGICAL WARDS, U.S.
ARMY HOSPITAL, CAMP ZAMA, JAPAN, 1969

Whatever else might be said about the Vietnam War, it was a medical success. During World War II, 30 percent of those wounded in combat died. In Korea because of the terrain, weather, distances involved, and lack of an efficient medical evacuation system, the percentage was substantially higher. The development of better surgical techniques, improved blood replacement, and rapid medevacs during Vietnam dropped the overall death rate to under 24 percent. Even more astonishing was the fact that of those wounded who did make it to a surgical or evacuation hospital less than 2.4 percent would not survive.

That astonishing survival rate, however, hid a basic fact. The majority of combat deaths in Vietnam occurred right on the front lines, before there was any chance or need of a medevac chopper. But if you were alive—even a little bit alive—when the chopper landed, you would in all likelihood survive. It was a reality not lost on those who fought the war.

Vietnam was clearly not World War II or Korea. The majority of both casualties and deaths in those wars were due to artillery. The deaths in Nam were much more close-up affairs. The North Vietnamese and the Vietcong could see you, knew where you were or, more than likely, where you would be going.

The ambushes, increasing lethality of weapons, and close-up use of rocket-propelled grenades, booby traps, and pressure-detonated mines were all aspects of Vietnam that proved so deadly.

In many ways, Vietnam was a turn right or step a bit to the left and you'd live, turn left or drag a foot and you were dead. In Nam, one moment you could be alive and the next you were dead.

But if the bleeding could be stopped and you were still breathing when they put you on a chopper, the odds were in your favor that you would survive. The soldiers understood that, no matter how grievous the wounds, if a medic could keep you alive until you were put on a chopper, you'd most likely make it home.

And because that much of the war was understood, because the combat troops knew it, because the officers encouraged it, and the medics believed it, "Keep 'em alive until the medevac comes in" became its own mantra and like all mantras, quickly became its own reality. In both theory and fact, someone in the Ninth Division fighting in the Mekong Delta or a trooper in the First Air Cavalry wounded in Vietnam's Central Highlands was no more than ten minutes away from a surgical facility. Both the mantra and the reality were simple enough: keep the wounded alive and they would stay alive. In 1969, while stationed at the U.S. Army Hospital in Camp Zama, Japan, taking care of the wounded medevaced from Vietnam, I wrote of the medics:

> At Zama we read in the stateside papers that America was going to hell, that it was almost impossible to get an American teenager to act responsibly, listen to an adult, or, for that matter, even to care. You'd think then, that it would be impossible to get them to kill themselves for something as vague as duty or run through claymores for anything as subtle as concern. But during the first five hours of Hamburger Hill, fifteen medics were hit, ten were killed. There was not one corpsman left standing. The 101st had to combat assault in medics from two other companies, and by nine that night, every one of them, too, had been killed or wounded.

There has always been an implicit sense of practicality to Americans. It was something Alexis de

Tocqueville noted in his travels through the United States in 1831–32 and remains today a part of our national character. Americans will always do what works whatever the sacrifice. And in Vietnam, it lead to a kind of bravery and self-sacrifice that became as commonplace as it was scary. The medics in Vietnam did what they did without orders and without complaint because they understood that minutes did matter and that keeping soldiers alive until the choppers came in did work.

There is a little-known secret about this selflessness that forced the Army in 1969 to change its rules about how long medics could stay out in the field. In early 1968, a report issued out of MACV(Military Assistant Command Vietnam) in Saigon documented that if current casualty rates among medics continued, there would be no medics left alive in any of the combat units by the end of their tours of duty. The rules were changed and from 1969 on, medics were only to spend six months on line before being rotated back to a battalion or base medical facility to finish off their tours of duty.

At a time when dissent was becoming a way of life and rebellion growing into an attitude, the continuing courage and self-denial of the medics were an extraordinary thing to witness. Even in an army slowly abandoned out at the edge of empire, the medics successfully struggled to keep their own alive.

Looked at objectively, what the medics did in Vietnam was not all that sophisticated. No one expected the medics to devise a comprehensive treatment plan or make any detailed medical assessments. In a way it was a little more than Boy Scout stuff: pack the wounds, stop the bleeding, maintain blood pressures, and keep everyone breathing until the medevac choppers flew in.

Courage, determination, sacrifice, and bravery made it all work, but the linchpin both emotionally and operationally of U.S. combat medicine was the anticipation and the reality of both a rapid and a timely evacuation of the wounded. And for the next twenty-five years, that was the standard of battlefield medical care. There was no thought of changing procedures, and certainly no thought of changing the training of combat medics.

But all that ended on the afternoon of October 3, 1993, when a search-and-rescue team rappelled down from a hovering helicopter into the streets of Mogadishu, Somalia. What should have been no more than a rescue mission protecting the distribution of foodstuffs by the United Nations to refugees of the Somali civil war had morphed through mission creep, into a search-and-destroy mission to capture or kill one of Somalia's major warlords. The "can-do" attitude of the military merged with the hubris of our government, to send an undermanned unit with a lack of armor and fire support to take on the Somalis in their own city, on their turf in the worst of all possible combat zones: the narrow streets and alleys of a crowded urban center.

Those U.S. Army Rangers and Special Forces troopers who fast-roped into Mogidishu quickly found themselves in a siege situation that would continue uninterrupted for almost two days, becoming the longest and deadliest firefight involving an American combat unit since the Vietnam War. The battle fought in those narrow streets and alleys was to change everything in both the theory and practice of combat medicine.

The minute-by-minute specifics of the battle are described by journalist Mark Bowden, in his *Blackhawk Down*. During what was really an eighteen hour gunfight, eighteen Rangers and Special Forces troopers were killed, two helicopters were shot down, dozens of other Americans soldiers were wounded. Hundreds of Somalis were wounded and killed. What had begun as a simple search-and-arrest operation had quickly become a desperate firefight for survival.

The medics, who along with the Rangers, rappelled down to the first crash site, came under intense fire the moment they hit the ground. Several members of the rescue team were hit while the medics, a number wounded themselves, had to deal with more and more casualties as the battle continued. Astonishingly, U.S. troops were sent to Somalia without armor. The Pentagon forgot one of the major rules of modern-day warfare—armored units are necessary for long-term survival. Apparently neither the Department of Defense nor the Joint Chiefs of

Staff thought there would be any prolonged battles or that tanks and armored personnel carriers would be necessary. The siege of U.S. troops was lifted only after the American command was able to borrow armored personnel carriers from Pakistani units on the other side of the city.

Through that first afternoon and night, the next day and the next night, until early the next morning, the medics had no choice but to care for the increasing numbers of wounded on their own. Additional choppers could not get in to reinforce the surrounded troops, nor could the medics get the casualties out.

In the words of one of the medics, "I gave IV fluids to people who had uncomplicated gunshot wounds in the arms and legs. They were fine, but I wasted time starting IVs and I wasted fluids, and then when I had someone with a pretty significant vascular injury, I was out of fluids. What we did was stupid . . . "

There is a maxim in the military that "you fight the way you train." What happened in Somalia was not stupid so much as out-of-date. While no one was looking, the kind of wars we had begun to fight had changed. Somalia was not World War II or Korea or even Vietnam; nor was Mogadishu Anzio, Kay Sahn, or Hue. Up until the Pentagon sent U.S. troops into Somalia, medics had simply been training for the past.

But in the setting of urban warfare, where choppers are at even greater risk than ground troops, the medical practices that had begun in World War II and been fine-tuned in Vietnam—maintaining airways, stopping bleeding, giving intravenous fluids to maintain vascular volumes and blood pressures, all focused on the goal of a rapid and effective medical evacuation—suddenly proved worthless.

Within hours of fast-roping into the streets of Mogadishu, the medics had used up all their IVs, all their plasma, all their tourniquets, and all their morphine, leaving nothing for the wounded they could not get out and nothing for the increasing numbers of new casualties coming in. It was not the training that had lost its effectiveness, it was the battlefield that had changed.

Mogadishu was the tipping point, that final wake-up call, forcing the military to abandon the last of its practices from Vietnam, its care of the wounded. The 1991 Persian Gulf War never really tested the established medical doctrine of stabilization of casualties followed by rapid chopper evacuations. There was no need. That war was fought out in the open, with half a million troops spread through five heavy divisions and dozens of armored battalions with complete battlefield and air superiority—all focused, as then Chairman of the Joint Chiefs of Staff General Colin Powell explained at the first press conference after the start of the war, on a single task: "Finding the enemy, fixing them in place and killing them." The war lasted only a few hundred hours, with fewer than 300 U.S. casualties.

But then came Mogadishu in 1993 and Kosovo in

1999 and half a dozen other military interventions. The rules were changing. To achieve its goals, our government was becoming more predisposed toward military options than diplomacy. U.S. presidents, as heads of our executive branch, were growing increasingly more willing to send troops into all kinds of circumstances in every corner of the world, using smaller and more agile units to fight in even more difficult terrain, the majority of actions behind enemy lines or along very long and sparsely defended supply routes. There was now little chance of the wounded being medevaced in a timely fashion. Medics would clearly have to learn a new trade. They would have to be able to keep casualties alive, without the possibility of evacuation, for up to seventy-two hours. It was time to change from triage to intensive care.

The training period for the Combat Medical Specialty was increased from ten to sixteen weeks. The former 91B military occupational specialty of Combat Medic was reclassified 91W (Health Care Specialist). All trainees were required to pass the civilian Emergency Medical Technician (EMT) test. The additional weeks of training were devoted to developing the new core skills necessary to keep the severely wounded alive where they were hit, with little chance for immediate evacuation. No more "patch 'em up and send them off." This was to be big-time medicine, the city trauma center brought to the battlefield.

The training added hands-on courses using high-tech patient simulators that could accurately mimic battlefield injuries, from respiratory failure to penetrating head wounds and transected spinal cords—in real time and under combat conditions. A "bleeding lab" set up to duplicate any number of hemorrhaging wounds became part of the program. The models used in the training actually would "bleed to death" if the blood loss was not stopped. The simulations are so real that the dummies really do "suffocate" if the chest tubes are not correctly placed or a tracheostomy performed within the required three minutes.

The military also incorporated the most recent and relevant advances in trauma surgery into the medical training. The evolving intensive-care theory of hypotensive resuscitation, where IV fluids are given only in minimal amounts solely to keep the heart pumping, rather than the old Vietnam method of resuscitation where blood pressures were maintained at normal or elevated levels, has become part of the teaching protocols, as well as one of the new standards of battlefield care.

In a tragic and ironic way, these new medical and surgical procedures work better with combat injuries than with civilian gun-shot wounds and car accidents. Combat troopers are basically healthy young men and women up until the time they are hit. In these patients, you can sacrifice a little blood pressure in order to keep forming blood clots from "popping loss" when blood pressures are raised too quickly or kept above normal levels too long.

Hypotensive resuscitation allows early clots to stay in place and new clots to form. But hypotensive blood and fluid replacement has an additional value on the battlefield. The large, cumbersome bottles and bags of plasma and IV fluids needed under the old techniques have been replaced by high-tech starch concentrate solutions, allowing medics to haul around fewer medical supplies while at the same time being able to care for more casualties. Better-designed tourniquets, along with the hemostatic embedded dressings and stints, have also been introduced for better local hemorrhage control.

Today's medics are taught to give antibiotics earlier and in much larger dosages than in the past. The deeper and more extensive the wounds, the greater the risk of infection. Medics are also taught to use the latest non-opioid pain-killers that, unlike morphine and Demerol, do not depress respiration. There is no doubt that today's medics can, if they have to, keep casualties alive for days, until that chopper or relief arrives. It is simply more difficult to die today than it was in Vietnam or Mogadishu. But there is more.

Part of today's survival is a result of the new body armor. Almost no one wore bullet-proof vests in Vietnam. It wasn't that Vietnam was hot; Afghanistan and Iraq are hot. It was that the vests didn't work well. They didn't cover enough of the body. They didn't stop the fully jacketed AK-47 rounds and for the most part didn't protect soldiers from mortars, antipersonnel mines or shrapnel.

Today's twenty-first century body armor is made up of a combination of ceramic plates and Kevlar. The new vests are lighter and more flexible than the 1960s-era vests, and they cover more of the trunk and torso. During the search for Osama Bin Ladin, a Special Forces trooper was shot at close range. Rounds from an AK-47 hit him in the chest. The trooper dropped to the ground, but a few moments later rose up again to shoot and kill his attacker. According to those who were there, it was like seeing Lazarus rise from the dead. Only this Lazarus rose up with an m-4 still in his hand. It was something that simply had never happened in any other war. Today's more effective body armor, which better protects the chest, heart, lungs, back, and upper abdomen, is part of the new survivability. But both the country and casualties have paid an unexpected and unanticipated price for all this success.

In a way, we have been lulled by our own success into a strange kind of reverie. Despite the growing sophistication of our battlefield medicine and the new body armor, the orthopedic wards at Walter Reed are becoming filled with numbers of amputees not seen since the Civil War, while more and more beds are being added to the neurosurgery and neurology units.

There is some argument today among military historians as to whether we really defeated Saddam's army in the field in 2003 or that some 400,000 Iraqi troops simply took off their uniforms and went home with their weapons, angry and without a job. What is clear is that as the war turned into an insurgency, the combatants aware of the overwhelming fire power of the U.S. military and the effectiveness of the troops' body armor gave up direct confrontations. They stepped up their use of IEDs, choosing support troops and supply convoys rather than the more heavily armed, protected, and aggressive combat units.

When our military added more armor to the units moving through hostile areas, the insurgents switched to the more powerful car bombs while increasing the power and blast radius of their IEDs. Unlike all our other wars, today's injuries, rather than coming from ahead and above, are coming from behind, below, and from the sides. Regular Army combat units and National Guard and Reserve troops started losing arms and legs and suffering head injuries at unexpected and unanticipated rates. Overwhelmed by the increasing numbers of mangled limbs, eye injuries, penetrating head wounds, and closed head trauma, the upgraded medical training following Mogadishu began to lose its edge.

Yet, despite the severity and grievousness of today's injuries, death rates have not increased, and even dropped compared with our other wars. The explosive charges that blew off arms and legs in Vietnam and Somalia killed those troops. The penetrating chest wounds, ruptured aortas, shattered livers and spleens, transected spinal cords, and fractured kidneys—along with the collapsed lungs and the massive internal hemorrhages that had always gone along with severe extremity wounds and head injuries—proved quickly fatal. The casualties with mangled or lost limbs and those with brain and spinal cord trauma never made it to the hospital. But that is no longer the case.

Military surgeons familiar with Vietnam speak with amazement that when they remove the body armor of today's medevacs, there is not a scratch from the chin to the groin and yet the arms and legs are mangled and the facial and head injuries horrific.

But nothing in war is ever as simple or as straightforward as it first appears. Surviving the terrible wounds of this war is not solely the result of better body armor and improved training for medics. Casualties survive today because the medical system itself has become more mobile and more agile. This war, under the Rumsfeld Doctrine of "Faster, Lighter, More Lethal," with its limited number of "boots on the ground"and widely dispersed units shuffled from border to border and town to town, along with the increasing severity of wounds, demanded a more sophisticated medical support that moved forward with the different units, a system that went beyond the post-Mogadishu "keep them alive for seventy-two hours" doctrine. Out of both common sense and the need to support a faster and lighter military, the Army devised and instituted a new upgraded concept of frontline battlefield medical care: Forward Surgical Teams, or FSTs.

These teams are in essence the MASH (mobile army surgical hospital) units of the Korean War era, only smaller and more nimble and in a strange way better equipped for their one specific task: survival. The typical team consists of fewer than twenty medical personnel: three general surgeons, one orthopedic surgeon, two nurse anesthetists, three nurses, and a few medics. Each FST travels in six Humvees. The transport vehicles carry three RATs (rapid assembly tents) that can be set up in fewer than sixty minutes and attached to each other to form a 900-foot surgical facility.

These are decidedly lean facilities. There is no high-tech radiographic equipment. Surgeons detect fractures by feel, but there are operating tables, ultrasonic equipment, and modern anesthesia packs, as well as high-tech ventilators.

These mobile units are not based on the major trauma centers that led to the EMT training of combat medics. These FSTs aim only for "damage control." There is no effort at definitive repair. The FST surgeon seeks to limit all operations to less than two hours, preferably to less than an hour. Abdomens are left open, bowels left unattached or connected to large drains, liver wounds simply packed to control bleeding, dirty wounds washed out, torn and useless bones and tissues removed.

The efficiency of the new system, as well as the resulting survival rates, are quite extraordinary, exceeding those of Vietnam. In Nam, the average time from the battlefield to the States was forty-five days; the average time now from Mosul or Nasharia to Landstuhl is twenty-four hours and on to Walter Reed or Bethesda Naval Hospital is less than four days. More importantly, even the number of those who did not survive after they reached a surgical facility, the 2.4 percent during the Vietnam War, has decreased. But in Iraq and Afghanistan, survival no longer gives the entire picture.

Numbers

"Armies are fragile institutions, and for all their might, easily broken." —JOE GALLOWAY

I t is not the devil, but the truth, that is in the details. Deaths have traditionally been viewed as a measure of potential victory or personal danger in any military conflict. With our current war in Iraq, the number of U.S. dead is now more than 2,400. The Pentagon and those who have championed this war have used the relatively small number of deaths compared with the number of troops at risk as a sign not only of how well we are doing but of the limited risk faced by our combat and support units.

But in this war the use of death as a function of peril is not only deceptive, it's delusional. Death in Iraq is no longer the real measure of risk. The story of this war cannot be told solely in the count of its dead. Whatever else may be said about the wars in Iraq and

Afghanistan, they are more wars of cripples and dis-abilities than they are wars of death.

"We were driving off the base to buy a few cans of soda from the peddlers on the street. A hand grenade came through the window and landed on the radio between me and my buddy who was driving. I could see the spoon was gone and a little smoke was coming out the top. Just as I grabbed for it, my buddy hit the gas and rammed the truck in front of us, trying to get us out of there. The grenade fell between my legs on the floor. I grabbed for it again and had it six inches off the ground when it exploded."

* * *

"My vehicle hit a mine and I lost my right leg just below the knee and broke my arm and ankle."

* * *

"The hatch to the APC was open and the sarge was look-ing around when a sniper shot him in the neck."

* * *

"The gunmen fired on our patrol from a passing car . . . "

* * *

"This guy stepped out from a side street, shouted, 'God is great!' and started firing an assault rifle."

* * *

"The roadside bomb exploded about 300 meters from our main base in Tikrit, Saddam's hometown, and then the next day two other guys were wounded when some mortar rounds hit our base . . . they were just showing us they were there."

44

* * *

"We were in a convoy, and all of a sudden . . . boom . . . the truck in front of us was blown off the road . . . they must have used a cell phone to set off the explosive charge."

No military likes to advertise their failures, nor their weakness, but the present U.S. administration has proved particularly reticent to dwell on the very existence of casualties—whether in its reluctance to allow photographs of caskets returning home or its objections to TV programs in which the names of the dead are read. But the numbers of wounded are virtually never mentioned and on those rare occasions when those numbers are released, no details are given as to types or severity of the injuries or to the causes, whether friendly fire, lack of adequate body armor, or vehicles that have not been properly up-armored.

But the real risk of this war can't be hidden. As of November 2004, there were 10,726 casualties. By the time you read this, the number of wounded will be well over 20,000. And more importantly, 80 percent will be the result of IEDs and roadside bombs that are becoming more sophisticated and more powerful every month.

A close reading of the data released by the Department of Defense indicates that approximately 6 percent of those wounded are amputees. By itself, this is twice the percentage of any of our past military conflicts, with foot and leg amputations being slightly more common than amputations involving the upper extremities. The number of amputees as a percentage of the wounded has not been so high among American troops since the first years of the Civil War.

"The nature of the trauma that we're seeing in this kind of deployment has to do with the fact that they have protective gear that allows them to survive, but it leads to a disproportionate number of limb loss injuries and multiple limb loss injuries."

But even the released data on amputations is somewhat deceiving. Not all limb injuries result in immediate amputation. Wherever possible, military surgeons practice "limb salvage" to save extremities. But limb salvage techniques, with multiple procedures of skin and vascular grafts, placement of internal rods, and muscle group transfer procedures, are not always successful. It may take up to two years before the surgeons and the patient give up and settle for an amputation.

What is also new about this war is the relatively high percentage of upper extremity injuries. Fifteen percent of amputees have lost both arms and legs and are in need of the more complicated and expensive prosthesis, as well as longer-term orthopedic support and medical care. And of course, there are the late deaths. Because of the heavy contamination of blast wounds from dirt, dust, and debris, casualties develop infections with what are now labeled "multi-resistant microorganisms." Many of the wounded have gone on to die of sepsis. These deaths, though, are not listed as primarily battlefield deaths. Military surgeons are also seeing unexpected rates of deep vein thrombosis, along with pulmonary embolus, among long-term survivors. The development of these clots is most likely due to the severity of the extremity injuries. If these complications eventually result in a fatal event, the deaths are not listed as a primary battlefield-related death.

While the numbers and types of casualties might be ignored, the truth of this war is much closer to the comment of a nurse at the Twenty-eighth Combat Surgical Hospital in Baghdad. "We're saving more people that shouldn't be saved. We're saving severely injured people, legs, eyes, parts of brains. These injuries are horrific."

Yet as devastating as the immediate injuries of the Iraq War might be, it is the long-term effects and medical costs that are truly staggering. There is an economics to survival. Care for the disabled takes personnel, effort, and money. It is a cost that never goes down to zero and goes up each year.

An above-the-knee computerized limb prosthesis, made of graphite and titanium, battery-powered, with servo systems built in for better movement and sway control, costs $50,000. That is not for the installation or maintenance—just the hardware. A below-the-knee prosthesis costs between $10,000 and $15,000, even without the constant attention and ongoing adjustments needed to keep the prosthesis operational. The military offers three types of upper-extremity prostheses: externally powered, body powered, and cosmetic. The three different prostheses, taken together, cost a total of $250,000 per patient. And that is only the beginning.

A limbless patient fitted with a prosthesis is a patient for life. Additional problems and new complications will inevitably arise with age and wear. Someone will have to pay and continue to pay or the wounded of this war will have to go without.

So what are the real costs of going to war in Afghanistan and Iraq. Right now, the majority of casualties, certainly the amputees and severe head injuries are kept within the Department of Defense's military hospital system—embedding the costs inside a mammoth military budget of some $500 billion annually. The DOD can and does pay for everything; DOD physicians routinely order same-day MRIs and CAT scans of the head and neck. DOD surgeons order all the prostheses. The DOD hospital system recently opened an amputee care center at Brooke Army Medical Center at Fort Sam Houston, Texas, that provides state-of-the-art care for service members who have lost limbs in Iraq and Afghanistan. In addition, a new multimillion-dollar, 29,000-square-foot amputee training facility is being built at Walter Reed. There are also plans for increasing DOD medical system's neurological and neurosurgical capabilities.

But the wounded stay within the DOD military health-care system only as long as they remain on active duty. Every wounded soldier will sooner or later become a veteran and will—unless he or she is old enough for Medicare or miraculously lucky enough to find a managed health-care company that will take on patients with extreme preexisting conditions—be forced to receive any ongoing care through the U.S. Department of Veterans Affairs. There is little to suggest that the VA—an overburdened and underfunded system—can handle the wounded from Iraq and Afghanistan once they are released from Department of Defense care.

The VA currently serves 7 million of the country's 25 million veterans. Today the average wait for a VA decision on an initial claim for disability benefits is 165 days; to rule on an appeal of one of its decisions, the VA takes, on average, three years. It is true that in the last ten years, some 13,700 veterans have died waiting for their cases to be resolved. In Minneapolis, the waiting period for an orthopedic appointment at the VA hospital can be more than six months, and patients there have been told to expect a further decrease in services over the next budget period. The VA needs more money, and its claims and appeals process needs an overhaul. Yet the Bush administration has refused to increase funding to the VA and has made no accommodations to deal with the influx of new veterans from Iraq. Of the 290,000 veterans of Iraq and Afghanistan who had left active duty by January 2005, 22 percent have already sought treatment from the VA; more than a quarter of them were diagnosed with some form of mental disorder in addition to their physical injuries. And the numbers of those seeking medical, surgical and psychological help is only expected to increase as the war drags on.

The increasing consequences of this war both in human terms and natural treasure are becoming clearer each day. It has all happened before.

During the ten years of the Vietnam War, we never had enough troops on the ground, we never closed the borders, never totally secured the cities and towns, and never had a strategy to get out. We tried to train a South Vietnamese army to take over the fighting, yet that army lasted barely a year before it collapsed. In the end, 58,000 American troops were killed and more than 450,000 were wounded until with no end of casualties in sight, we simply had enough, gave up, and went home.

But perhaps the real tragedy is that this administration did not listen to Chief of Staff of the Army, General Frederick C. Weyland, in his own assessment, more than thirty years ago, of our ultimate failure in Vietnam:

> There is no such thing as a "splendid little war," there is no such thing as a war on the cheap. War is death and destruction. The Army must make the price of involvement clear before we get involved, so that Americans can weigh the probable costs of involvement against the dangers of involvement.

Essences

Things

General Fred C. Weyand pointed out the obvious in his famous 1976 analysis of U.S. Military Tactics and Strategy:

> The American way of war is a particularly violent, deadly and dreadful. We believe in using "things"—artillery, bombs, massive firepower—in order to conserve our soldiers' lives. The enemy, on the other hand, makes up for his lack of "things" by expending men instead of machines, and for that suffers enormous casualties. The army saw this happening in Korea, and we should have made the realities of [the Vietnam War] obvious to the American people before they

witness it on their television screens. What is clear is that this reliance on things goes way back. (CDRS Call, July–Aug., pp. 3–4)

Sometimes it works . . .

Following the Battle of the Bulge during World War II, a captain in General Patton's Third Army, which had broken through the German lines surrounding Bastogne, questioned one of the captive German officers and, clearly irritated by what he considered the officer's arrogance, challenged the German that if the Wehrmacht was such a superior fighting force, what were he and his men doing in a prisoner-of-war camp? "Well," the officer answered in perfect English, "We set up our guns. And you Americans sent a tank down our road and we destroyed it. Then you sent another tank down the same road and we destroyed that tank. Then you sent a third and fourth tank which we destroyed. Unfortunately, we ran out of ammunition before you Americans ran out of tanks."

Sometimes it doesn't . . .

"Things" didn't work so well in Korea. Despite artillery barrages and relentless round-the-clock air attacks, the Chinese were willing and did take enormous casualties as they drove the Eighth Army and the Marines back from the Yalu River into South

Korea. There were reports that some units of the Chinese army attacked with only pitchforks and axes.

And things, lots more things, didn't work in Vietnam. There is a recorded conversation held in Hanoi during the peace negotiations preceding our withdrawal from Southeast Asia: "You do know," explained an American officer to the Vietnamese negotiator, "that you never defeated us on the battlefield."

The North Vietnamese colonel pondered the remark for a moment. "That may be so," he answered carefully, "but it is also irrelevant."

No army wants to lose. Tactics, strategies, and weapon systems are always being shifted about and changed, if not to get an advantage, at least to survive. What is sure today is that conquest and success are not what they used to be and that victory can be no more than simply not losing.

Desperation is the real mother of invention, leading at times to what at first might appear to be desperate measures. In war, though, you use what is given to you. Whatever the final tactics though, if one side's price goes up, so will the other. In a strange but real way, modern warfare has all become a kind of crazed zero sum game.

Senior Lieutenant Colonel Nguyen Hu An, deputy commander of the B-3 Front and commanding officer of the sixty-six North Vietnam Regiment, made just that point in an interview thirty years after the first major battle between units of the Regular North Vietnamese Army and the technically advanced U.S.

First Air Cavalry using the new tactics of vertical envelopment:

> We had never fought the Americans and were curious about this use of helicopters, which our troops, because of the thumping noise, called tractors with propellers. During the battle, I sat out of the mountain and watched how the helicopters and aircraft were used in this new kind of war. It was very interesting.

What Colonel Hu An and other Vietnamese officers watched and appreciated and quickly grasped was that they could not match the massive firepower of the Americans. They understood that, in the last analysis, any prolonged battle with the ever-increasing use of long-range artillery, helicopter gunships, napalm, fighter bombers, and saturation B-52 raids would always tip the scale of victory toward the Americans. The Vietnamese realized that the only way their units could survive a firefight with the Americans was to get in close, to "grab the Americans by the belt buckle," and not let go, that to give up distance during an attack or firefight was in essence to lose the battle. The strategy was to get in close and stay close, whatever the costs.

It was a desperate policy, but in the give-and-take of war, it worked. Quick attacks, close-in ambushes, the breaking off of contact before gunships and fighter bombers arrived, became the North Vietnamese ways of neutralizing both American technology and American firepower. It was, of course, not so much a way to win as a way not to lose. No small thing when the only other alternative is simply take it and die in place.

What the Vietnamese had learned and then put into place would become painfully clear over the remaining ten years of the Vietnam War. Large unit attacks were to be avoided. The American units might pound them, but the Vietnamese could, by picking the time and place of their battles, getting in close to offset the offensive firepower, and then withdrawing as quickly as possible after initial contacts, make up for being outgunned while bleeding the Americans at their own game. For the Vietnamese, the war was not to be a sprint but a marathon.

Despite the enormous superiority in equipment, the military was to pay a very high and eventually politically unsustainable price for Vietnam. The years following Vietnam were a desperate time for the military. James Kitfield, in his 1995 book, *Prodigal Soldiers: How the Generation of Officers Born of Vietnam Revolutionized the American Style of War*, deals with those years and the few courageous officers who at great personal sacrifice and professional ridicule stayed in the military to reinvent and reconstitute an Army no longer crippled by the effect of the Vietnam War nor challenged and abused by those it was pledged to protect.

Those officers focused on reestablishing morale within the military, the confidence of the country in its armed forces, and a professionalism among the officers and enlisted ranks. The "Be the Best You Can Be" came out of that era of rebuilding, as did a more defined role for committing the Army, Air Force, and Marines. The history of our military during the late 1970s and 1980s was one of refinement of strategy, tactics, and force structure. Vietnam was not to be ignored so much as not repeated. Those officers who stayed on formed the nucleus of a military that would, twenty-five years after its collapse in Vietnam, take on and beat Saddam Hussein's Republican Guards in less than a hundred hours during Desert Storm, our first Persian Gulf War.

Part of the new focus was on increasing lethality, but the blueprint for the reformation was a military able to defeat any army anywhere in the world. All of this was supported by the Weinberger-Powell doctrine put into place by Secretary of Defense Casper Weinberger and Secretary of State Colin Powell as a response to the errors of Vietnam: no war without putting into place overwhelming force, no war without a commitment from the whole country, no war without a well-defined goal and appropriate exit strategy.

Finally, after two decades, our military had both regrouped and reorganized. The military had sought ways to innovate, to establish a more effective command and control, and to become more lethal. The Army, Air Force, Marines, and Navy developed the ability to retask combat assets in real time, to find ways of increasing strike capabilities to bring more firepower to bear at those points where maximum force was necessary. There were adaptations to what military theorists had begun to call the new realities of asymmetrical warfare—in more technical terms, the extension of the battlefield in both time and space. In reality, an army in the field can only do two things: break things and kill people. The object of any army is to do one or both better, quicker, and more efficiently than any other army.

Colonel Douglas A. Macgregor, in his 1997 monograph *Breaking the Phalanx*, recommended a reconfiguration of combat units to ensure more mobility and flexibility while giving units the ability to concentrate overwhelming force at the precise time and the exact point of engagement. Macgregor understood that we are a technologically advanced and innovative nation and that those qualities should be brought to bear on the problem of military efficiency and effectiveness. Mogadishu was not only a shock to the Army Medical Corps, but to the whole U.S. military. Without armor and with the vulnerability of helicopters to the close-in fighting of urban warfare, a firefight was really gunmen against gunmen. In those battles, the side with the most gunmen usually wins. No one wanted that to happen again.

Smart bombs in the form of satellite-guided munitions, that can be sent through the second-floor windows of a four-story building or take out a single truck on a bridge, reactive armor on tanks, Advance Combat Optical Gunsights (ACOG) optical sights and night-vision goggles, "fire and forget" weapons, real-time battlefield communication, and the integration of artillery with close-in air support were all parts of the new transformation.

The development and availability of reliable satellite-guided munitions that could be used with astonishing accuracy and precision, whatever the weather—in fog or mist, in the middle of the darkest night, even in sandstorms—allowed smaller, faster units, carrying light equipment and moving quickly, to overcome larger forces. The concentration of enemy formations, whatever their size, configuration, or force structure, was no longer an issue. And it worked.

There was an incident at the beginning of the Afghan war where a single Special Forces unit, using handheld GPS locators, called in air strikes on hundreds of Taliban fighters blocking the passes out of the northern mountains. The Afghans, used to a decade of ineffectual Russian carpet bombing, watched as U.S. F-16s dropped satellite-guided, 500-pound bombs to within meters of their own positions. It was a touchy time for all concerned. More than one uncommitted Afghan tribal chief, having watched the precision bombing that allowed the breakout onto the plains of northeastern Afghanistan, decided then and there that they wanted to be on the side of these new guys. It was indeed an example of "Shock and Awe."

By the end of the 1990s, it could truly be said of our army what Wellington had said of his Highland Light Infantry before the battle of Waterloo: "I do not know if they frighten the enemy, but they certainly frighten me."

In a way, we might have gotten too good at war. Our weapons have become more deadly, our tanks more powerful, our bombs more precise, our new modern personal body armor more protective. But technology does not guarantee victory. What technology gives, technology can also hide, or worse, give away.

And sometimes we forget . . .

The Bush administration took the country into Iraq with the world's most powerful military. It pushed for even a "faster, quicker, lighter" force structure supported by even more lethal "on demand" fire power. The Rumsfeld Pentagon dismissed past experiences as no longer important or relevant. Yet the need for survivability was known to the military architects who proposed this smaller more agile military but those in the Bush administration chose to ignore that aspect of military doctrine. Colonel Douglas A. Macgregor, in his 2003 book *Transformation Under Fire: Revolutionizing How America Fights*, warned about the need for survivability once an army is set loose on an enemy force:

> When American light infantry is armed
> with automatic weapons and the enemy

has automatic weapons, any resistance
encountered is stiff because conditions of
symmetry prevail. When these conditions
emerge, the light infantry turns to the
must powerful weapon in its inventory—
the radio, because it allows them to call
for help from the air force, the navy and
the artillery.

Without the ability to deploy air assets or the availability of sufficient quantities of armored equipment
to use as stable and protected weapons platforms,
lightly armed units moving through enemy territory
are always in danger. Macgregor makes the statement that whatever the situation, "when significant
armor arrives on the scene, the battle ends quickly."

But concern about the ability to endure as well as
survivability has not only been ignored but dismissed. The Rumsfeld Pentagon ordered many of the
original armored divisions going to Iraq to leave
more than half of their tanks and Bradley Fighting
Vehicles at home—in reality turning tank and
artillery crews into light infantry, sent out in under-
armored transport vehicles to patrol the deadliest
roads in the world.

The one clear sign of insanity is to do the same
thing over and over again and expect different
results. The most recent combat units sent to Iraq
left the States without having their vehicles adequately up-armored. Up-armored means the addi-

tion of welded thick armored plate to protect troopers riding in vehicles that without the armor, cannot protect those inside from the roadside blast effects of a series of linked 155-millimeter shells wrapped in nails, or the focused impact of a car filled with cylinders of butane and five hundred pounds of high explosives. Effective body armor is the last level of personal protection, whether a crusader's breast plate deflecting a flight of Saracen arrows or a Rhode Island National Guardsman in a truck or Humvee hoping that there is not a roadside bomb around the next corner.

But it is not only vehicles. In January '06, a secret Pentagon study, reported in the *New York Times*, classifying the types of wounds and causes of death in Marines, found that 80% of those Marines killed in Iraq from March '03 to June '05, most likely would have survived if they had been wearing the wider, more-effective body armor. In 70% of these deaths, the issue was high-velocity projectiles, mainly bullets, that had penetrated around the ceramic plates set in place to protect the torso. Even more troubling was the fact that approximately 30% of these fatal wounds struck the chest, sides, and backs of these Marines so close to the protective plates that according to the study, "simply enlarging the existing shields" would have had the potential to alter the fatal outcomes. Additional forensic studies by the Armed Forces Medical Examiner Unit obtained by the *New York Times* documented that some 340 of those soldiers killed in Iraq and Afghanistan died specifically from torso wounds.

Virtually from the beginning of this war, troopers have been asking for additional protection to at least stop bullets from "slicing through their sides." Some soldiers have even begun readjusting their own body armor, hanging the crotch protector plates under their arms to cover those open areas that their vest does not protect.

The Pentagon, for reasons that seem unfathomable, has been slow and even reluctant to expedite the armoring of our vehicles as well as the up-armoring of our troops. In more than one combat or support unit, parents and relatives personally buy and send the available and more protective body armor to their sons and daughters on active duty in Iraq and Afghanistan. Everyday throughout the war zones, troopers climb into their poorly armored trucks and Humvees and leave their base camps simply hoping they will return alive.

In any war, weaknesses soon become apparent and can always be expected to be exploited. Iraq is no different from Vietnam or any of our other wars. The enemy uses roadside bombs, ambushes, suicide bombers, and car bombs not only because they work but because they are all they have.

We have a military that could level any city or town in Iraq in a few days and destroy or cripple any division of enemy troops caught out in the field within a few hours. But that is no longer the war we are fighting and might never have been. Like, Vietnam something has gone terribly wrong. In a war where a quick, painless success was virtually assured, our troops—inadequately protected for the war they are fighting, spread too thin, only partially armored, overworked, and worn down—are paying the price for a battlefield that our leaders refuse to acknowledge and that the war apologists pretend is not even there . . .

Final Diagnosis

"Every soldier killed in action gets an autopsy, or at least an external exam. It is one of the rules. All that changes is how they are injured and how they die . . . "

—PATHOLOGIST, U.S. ARMY HOSPITAL, CAMP ZAMA, 1969

Vietnam 1969:

The Chinese mines the Vietnamese use are made of plastic. They contain five to ten pounds of explosives and are virtually invisible to metal detectors. These mines are pressure-detonated, the explosive charge rigged to go off for any set weight—a tank, a jeep, or a truck. These explosives can disable a truck or blow a track off an armored personnel carrier. When the Vietnamese have enough mines to waste, they set them up for patrols and to ambush recon teams. If they are placed just right, the mines can take down most of a squad. For sure, they will kill anyone within a half-dozen meters.

This one blew as soon as the trooper stepped on it. Those who were there said that they heard the pop as soon as he stepped off the trail, and the next second there was this blinding flash and rush of hot air. The trooper was unconscious before the medics reached him and dying as the medevac chopper landed. The chopper took him to the Twenty-seventh Surgical Hospital near Quang Tri, where they amputated what was left of his right leg, removed both testicles, explored his abdomen, took out his left kidney and four inches of large bowel, sewed up his liver, and did a colostomy and right ureterostomy. During the procedure, he was given thirty units of uncrossed O-positive blood.

After two days at the Twenty-seventh, he was evacuated to Japan via the Yokota Air Base. From Yokota, he was taken by chopper to the U.S. Army hospital at Camp Zama. His left leg was removed by a left-hip disarticulation the day he arrived; a number of new chest tubes were placed to drain the accumulating pleural effusions. There was not enough skin to close all the wounds, so his stumps were left open. Despite antibiotics, the deeper wounds became infected. On the fourth day, urinary output began to drop, and the laboratory began culturing gram negative bacteria out of the patient's blood. On the sixth day, the patient's fever hit 106 degrees; he became delirious and then unconscious, and the next day the trooper died. The body was then transferred to the mortuary at Yokota, where an autopsy was performed.

Final Pathological Diagnosis
EXTERNAL EXAMINATION
The body is that of a well-developed, well-nourished,

though thin, Negro male in his late teens or early twenties, showing absence of both lower extremities and extensive blast injuries on the perineum. There is a large, eight-inch surgical incision running from the chest wall to the pubis. There is a previous amputation of the distal right thumb and left index finger.

DIAGNOSIS

1. Death, eight days after stepping on a land mine.
2. Multiple injuries:
   A. Traumatic amputation of lower extremities, distal right thumb, distal left index finger.
   B. Blast injury of anus and scrotum.
   C. Avulsion of testicles.
   D. Fragment wounds of abdomen.
   E. Laceration of kidney and liver, transection of left ureter.
3. Focal interstitial myocarditis and right heart failure.
   A. Left and right ventricular dilation.
   B. Marked pulmonary edema, bilateral.
   C. Marked pulmonary effusion, bilateral (3,000 cc in the left, 1,500 in the right).
   D. Congestion of lungs and liver.
4. Patchy acute pneumonitis (Klebsiella-Aerobacter organism).
5. Gram-negative septicemia.
6. Extensive acute renal tubular necrosis, bilateral.
7. Status post multiple recent surgical procedures:

A. Hip disarticulation with debridgement of stumps, bilateral.

B. Testicular removal bilaterally.

C. Exploration of abdomen, suturing of lacerated liver.

D. Removal of left kidney and ureter.

E. Multiple blood transfusions.

* * *

Iraq 2005:

Sergeant Maria Martinez's unit was ambushed in an attack that began in the early morning of the last day of summer in a town thirty miles west of Baghdad. Sergeant Martinez was in a "bucket," an unarmored Humvee with an open back, turning it into a small utility truck. Everyone knew that the vehicle was dangerously vulnerable to IEDs so a system had been put into place to rotate the troops who rode inside. Riding inside was at best an upgraded Iraqi version of Russian roulette. The day Martinez was in the Humvee, they'd added a layer of sandbags to the floorboards for protection. The roadside bomb was detonated by remote control. It went off just as the Humvee was slowing down to make a right-hand turn. The left side of the Humvee took the full force of the blast. The bomb had been placed inside the concrete curb, undetected until someone, probably waiting in a grove of palm trees, or hiding in a nearby house, set it off. The force of the blast was so great that it lifted the Humvee into the air. When they got to Sergeant Martinez, she was still alive. Emergency surgery was performed a half hour later in an FST and two hours later she was at the Twenty-fourth Combat Surgical Unit in Baghdad.

Final Pathological Diagnosis
EXTERNAL EXAMINATION

The body is that of a well-developed, well-nourished, Hispanic American in her early twenties, exhibiting the typical physical findings of a severe blast injury. There is obvious external head trauma with a dislocated jaw, enucleated left eye, and evulsed left maxillary sinus. There are numerous fragmentation wounds on the face and neck. The right leg and the left foot are missing, and there is evidence of second- and third-degree burns of the arms and hands. Despite a collapsed right lung, there are no marks, cuts, or abrasions on the trunk or torso from the chin down to the groin in areas known to be protected by body armor. The brain itself is markedly swollen, with areas of punctate hemorrhages over the cortex, along with extensive areas of bruising over the visual cortex and left frontal lobe.

Dignosis

1. Death from multiple blast injuries
2. Multiple injuries:
   A. Traumatic amputation right leg, left foot
   B. Traumatic amputation first two fingers left hand, thumb and forefinger right hand
   C. Fragmentation wounds of face and neck

D. Multiple skull fractures
   Dislocated right mandible
   Fracture right maxillary sinus
   Evulsion right globe
E. Significant close head brain trauma
3. Positive blood culture
   Septic shock
4. Status post multiple surgical procedures
   A. Deceased—multi-organ system failures.

* * *

More than 60 percent of casualties during World War II were due to artillery and mortars. In a way, these were indiscriminate wounds. It was much the same in Korea. In Vietnam, it was mostly booby traps, RPGs (Rocket Propelled Grenades), and close up automatic fire. It was all much more intimate and personal. You knew who was there and most likely could see or hear them. In Iraq and Afghanistan, injury and death is simply waiting and they are looking at you the whole time. Forget about the "Electronic Battlefield" and "Shock and Awe." The signature weapons of this war have become the suicide bomber and the roadside bomb.

Recently, Iraqi insurgents have begun to counter even up-armored vehicles by linking together 155-millimeter shells as well as using shaped charges specifically designed to penetrate armor. The White House and the Pentagon might insist that these weapons be called IEDs, or improvised explosive devices, but there is hardly anything "improvised" about a weapon that can blow a hole through an armored personnel carrier or turn over a twenty-six-ton amphibious assault vehicle. It is this kind of obfuscation that adds to the confusion about this war and that sense of political and military drift. The Pentagon should have realized from the very beginning that Iraq was no longer the war they had trained for nor expected when, during the race up to Baghdad, the largest number of casualties began to occur in support rather than frontline combat troops.

The refusal to accept—much less anticipate—the war we have been given, becomes glaringly clear with the whole issue of roadside bombs. Operationally, the question becomes where and how the insurgency is getting their explosives. The answer was clear from the beginning. Before the war even began, air and satellite surveillance had documented 600 ammunition dumps scattered throughout Iraq. There were never enough troops to adequately secure more than 25 percent of these dumps. Those remaining, some with tons of weapons, were and are still guarded by Iraqi police. The scenario that began with the toppling of Saddam Hussein's statue in Baghdad and continues today goes like this: a group of insurgents drives a truck up to the gate of an ammunition dump and gives the Iraqi guards two choices—a hundred dollar bill to let them into the dump, or death.

In 2005, virtually 100 percent of our deaths and 80 percent of our casualties were from roadside bombs. Along open stretches of highway or on the streets of towns and villages, our troops are at a loss to keep from being killed one and two at a time or wounded by the dozens.

But it is not only the availability of huge quantities of explosives that has made Iraq so dangerous; it is the new and devastating way these bombs do their damage. Today's IEDs result in three types of injuries. First, there are the wounds caused by projectiles, either set in motion by the explosive charge or pieces of the bomb itself. A second type of wound centers around extremity burns, as well as the damage to the lungs. Suffocation remains one of the many immediate fatal complications of blast injuries. Finally, there are those injuries related solely to the direct effects of the blast wave itself.

The majority of deaths still result from penetrating wounds of the head and neck or, despite body armor, from being impaled by high-velocity objects set in motion by the explosive charges. Virtually all bombs in Iraq contain metallic fragments—disintegrating shell casings as well as nails, nuts, and bolts packed around the shells or mortar rounds—additional fragments designed or used specifically to cause penetrating wounds. There are gaps in body armor below the waist and under the arms that leave the torso vulnerable to high-velocity missiles, while there remain areas of the head and neck not adequately protected from objects coming from below and from the side. Penetrating injuries from primary fragments (fragments that are part of the weapon itself) and secondary fragments (those that result from the explosion) are now the leading cause of immediate death and injury in the military as they are in civilian terrorist attacks.

Burns remain a significant source of injury in any war, and the cause even today of significant lifelong disabilities. Burns from explosive devices can be either chemical or thermal. Third-degree burns of more than 20 percent of the body carry the risk of overwhelming infection and death. Explosive devices, particularly those detonated in close proximity to vehicles can and do lead to what are called "flash burns" of the respiratory tract, resulting in respiratory impairment and, depending on the distance from the explosive charge, death from immediate asphyxiation. Toxic inhalants can also lead to persistent breathing disabilities, while carbon monoxide production—owing to either primary or secondary fires—can cause persistent brain damage.

The Pentagon, no longer able to ignore the obvious, has finally acknowledged that insurgents are killing and injuring more and more American troops with bigger and bigger bombs.

But if you survive the flying debris and penetrating wounds and the burns, there is still the blast itself. In this war, it is the blast waves themselves that cause the most damage and have made the injuries so unique and so deadly. Injuries from blast waves have proven the most problematical, the most disabling, and the most difficult to treat. As the war goes on, the roadside and car bombs are becoming more powerful and the bombings more frequent. And along with the increasing power and frequency of the bombing, these blast wave injuries are becoming more common.

The detonation of any powerful explosive device generates a blast wave of high pressure that spreads out from the point of explosion. The blast wave, whether out in the open or confined in a closed space, consists of an initial shock wave of very high pressure followed closely by what is called a "secondary wind," the result of the huge volume of displaced air flooding back into the area of the low pressure generated behind the wake of the original blast front. It is the sudden and extreme differences in pressures, particularly of the initial shock wave, that lead to organ damage. Military physicians have learned that significant blast injuries should be suspected in any soldier exposed to a blast, whatever the distance from the explosion.

However effective adequately armored vehicles or body armor might be in preventing penetrating wounds, they do not protect against injuries resulting from the shock waves of the primary blast. The force of the explosive charges in today's devices, particularly the larger bombs, can be so great that armor simply loses its effectiveness. The physics of this war has added a new dimension to battlefield casualties: wounds that are not easily seen. Soldiers are now dying who have no external signs of injury.

The high-explosive weapons being used in ever-increasing numbers with ever-increasing finesse and complexity in Iraq and Afghanistan have forced the military, and in particular military physicians, to adjust diagnosis and treatment to the new battlefield conditions and to these new types of injuries. For better and worse, there has been, by necessity, a very rapid learning curve.

Ear drums are blown out from as little as a five-pound-per-square-inch rise above atmospheric pressure. Exposures to less than a twenty-five-pound pressure per square inch rapid increase in pressure can dislocate the bones of the middle ear, leading to permanent hearing loss.

But hearing loss, while common, is one of the less critical issues. Pulmonary trauma is the most critical injury in troops close to a blast center. Following an explosion, there is no time for any part of the body to adjust to the sudden change in surrounding air pressures. The lungs are especially susceptible to pressure damage. A sudden, violent increase in air pressure can explode the air already in the lungs. Lungs can and do rupture and bleed from this kind of baro-trauma, especially if the explosion is confined to a small space or the detonation is close to an enclosed vehicle. Pneumothorax and pulmonary edema can be an instantaneous cause of death, while the leakage of air into the circulation through ruptured lungs will lead to emboli that can occlude blood vessels going to the brain and spinal cord, causing severe and life-threatening neurological damage.

Rupture of the colon, small intestine, and bladder can also occur from barotrauma. Hemorrhages into solid organs including the liver, spleen, and kidneys are also part of the effects of exposures to blast forces, the frequency of all such injuries increasing dramatically the closer the trooper is to the explosive charge.

Blast injuries to the eyes, while not life-threatening, result in a large percentage of wounds now being seen in both Iraq and Afghanistan. Pressure injuries to the eyes involve rupture of the eyeball itself, corneal lacerations, and traumatic cataracts, as well as damage to the optic nerves.

"The injured eye can be covered with a paper cup or other clean object that will not exert pressure. The patient can then be referred for definite surgical treatment. Chemical burns of the eye should be treated by at least sixty minutes of continuing irrigation with sterile saline . . . "

But it is the closed head injuries that have proven to be the most frequent and most challenging of these new blast injuries. There has been an astonishing increase in the number of closed head injuries compared with the incidence of such injuries during our other wars.

The concussive effects of a nearby 500-pound bomb or a series of linked 155-millimeter shells, surrounded by canisters of butane gas and detonating next to, or under a Humvee, a Bradley Fighting Vehicle, an armored personnel carrier or even a tank, is devastating to a trooper's central nervous system. The enormous force of the blast waves can cause severe and persistent damage. And those forces have grown stronger as the insurgents adapting to the armor of U.S. troops have begun to use shaped charges in their roadside bombs. These high-tech but easily constructed charges focus the energy of the blasts into a narrow, ultrahot plasma beam that can penetrate six inches of high-tension steel plate. These bombs have become so devastating that two years after the war began, commanders on the ground have begun to issue orders restricting the numbers of troops riding in armored vehicles in the hopes of holding down the numbers of casualties. But these shaped charges along with the more basic roadside and car bombs continue to cause neurological injuries that are as diverse as they are difficult to treat.

Primary injuries to the brain include concussions, resulting in loss of consciousness, and what neurologists had formerly called coup-contracoup injuries, a term formerly restricted to central nervous system injuries resulting from severe blows to the head. But with the increasing power of the car, truck, and roadside bombs, military physicians have discovered that damage to the central nervous system following an explosion can be attributable to the direct effects of the blast waves themselves.

In July 2005, it was estimated at Walter Reed Army Medical Center that two-thirds of all soldiers wounded in Iraq and not immediately returned to duty suffer from traumatic head injuries as well as their other wounds. Indeed, for the first time in all our wars, the military is treating more extremity and head injuries than chest or abdominal wounds. The numbers and complicated nature of the head injuries have forced the military to give a new term to these nonpenetrating head wounds: Traumatic Brain Injury, or TBI. Such injuries can cause massive brain swelling, leading to blindness, deafness, and severe mental retardation, as well as significant psychiatric and emotional problems.

The new U.S. German-style helmets with their raised earflaps may protect against some projectiles, but they are not designed to absorb the force of an explosion. In a blast, the weight of these helmets only adds to the injury. "It's like a pan on your head, held by a shoestring webbing," an Army combat engineer explained. "When you take a hit, it rings your head like a bell."

In truth, no helmet can defend against a wave front moving at 1,600 feet per second with a pressure gradient more than 1,000 times that of atmospheric pressure. In this war, the head has become one of the most vulnerable parts of the body.

"Blast injuries affect more widespread parts of the brain than the typical shell fragment injury . . . "

The Army's Thirty-first Combat Support Hospital in Baghdad, the only U.S. medical facility in Iraq with CAT-scan capability and neurosurgeons, regularly performs craniotomies—a procedure in which the skull is opened and the injured brain inside is examined. As a combat surgeon there, viewing the brain of a soldier, said of his work, "We can save you. You might not be what you were."

Indeed, soldiers walking away from blasts have later discovered that they suffer from memory loss, short attention spans, muddled reasoning, headaches, confusion, anxiety, depression, and irritability. In a 2004 article in *The Journal of Brain Injury*, entitled "Depression, Cognition and Functional Correlates of Recovery Outcome after Traumatic Brain Injury," neurologists acknowledge that patients with mild to moderate traumatic brain injuries are more affected by their emotional problems than by their residual physical disabilities. The article ends with an admonition that it is important to screen blast injury patients for depression and to conduct neuropsychological testing soon after a potential head injury in order to institute treatment and ensure a successful reentry into the civilian community.

Because of the decision to rely on Reserve and National Guard units to pursue this war, a large percentage of those with closed head injuries are not the eighteen- and nineteen-year-old Marines or combat troopers from the Third Infantry Division or the 101st Airborne, but are the substantially older husbands, wives, fathers, and mothers of the Minnesota, Louisiana, and Rhode Island National Guard. A TBI to a thirty-five-year-old with two children at home is a wound that affects the future of a whole family. For the majority of head injuries, there is the inability to concentrate, the emotional swings, depression and anxiety, the loss of a job. The economic and emotional instability of a family left can be as terrifying and as real as any difficulty focusing or simply waking at night crying. But the real concern is that significant closed head injuries are being underdiagnosed. Army neurologists fear that subtle but real neurological and related psychological problems are simply being missed in those troopers exposed to blasts but not visibly injured enough to enter the medical evaluation chain. A 2005 medical paper on casualties resulting from blasts cautioned that these injuries are "notorious for their delayed onset." In truth, very few are spared the blast effects of a car or roadside bomb. Indeed, that blast injuries to the brain should be expected in any soldier exposed to these explosions, regardless of the distance from the blast center. It is the newest legacy of this newest American war . . . and a legacy that is growing each month.

Shell Shock

"War is not an easy thing . . . "
　　　　　　　　—CONVERSATION: PSYCHIATRIC WARD,
　　　　　　　　U.S. ARMY HOSPITAL, CAMP ZAMA, JAPAN, 1969

During the early years of World War II, one of every four soldiers evacuated from a combat area was medevaced out as a neuropsychiatric patient, and fully half of the medical discharges granted at that time were granted for psychiatric disability. Whatever else might be said about the battlefield, it is a fearful place not only for the brain, but for the mind.

Still, no army is willing to admit the obvious—that war is a frightening and at times terrifying thing. Going into battle or being in a firefight that first time is difficult enough. Doing the same thing twice or three or four times can become an impossible task. It has been said that the Marines who survived Saipan in World War II and were on their way to Iwo Jima already thought of themselves as dead.

The Army understands that kind of dread and foreboding. The best of the field grade and general officers, remembering their own times on the front lines, continue to feel it themselves. It was clear to those who knew of General Norman Schwarzkopf's history as a twenty-four-year-old captain in Vietnam that his refusal during the 1991 Persian Gulf War to let the Marines land on the heavily mined beaches of Kuwait, using instead the amphibious forces solely as a decoy, was because of his own paralyzing experience in Vietnam, when on a second tour as a battalion commander in 1968, he entered a minefield to save a wounded soldier who had touched off a mine, and then painstakingly, had to work his way and that of his other troopers out of the half mile wide minefield.

When asked by a reporter at a press briefing following the first days of Desert Storm why he had not let the Marines come ashore, Schwarzkopf answered angrily, "Have you ever been caught in the middle of a minefield?"

Still, no army wants to lose its soldiers because of something as universal and yet as apparently vague and personal as fear. The military is not about individuals but the group. It is not that soldiers are afraid that troubles the military. Everyone who has been in a battle understands that much about war. What worries the military is that the individual fear might spread, or worse, become a reason for large numbers of troops simply to give up or refuse to go forward.

So, in the same way that they handled physical wounds so easily seen and even more easily understood, military leaders have always tried to dismiss the anxiety and desperation of the battlefield, too, as something that is physical; something that *happens* to soldiers; something that is real, not anything fanciful or something that soldiers do to themselves, and more importantly not something that might spread.

During the Civil War, the first great war after the Industrial Revolution, where death and destruction was on an industrial scale, those soldiers either unwilling or unable to continue, who seemed lost in the middle of all the bloodshed and slaughter, or those who survived and went home only to remain distant and angry, or who woke up in the middle of the night screaming, were said to be suffering from an "Irritable Heart." No need for magic here; no need to conjure up malingering, satanic possessions, or cowardice; no need for embarrassment. The problem, whatever the symptoms, was clearly physical—the end result of an overstimulated heart.

In World War I, that diagnosis was changed. By 1915, those shaken and trembling soldiers removed from the brutality of the trenches were diagnosed as "Shell Shocked," the focus shifting from the heart to the brain and central nervous system. Even to the most casual observer, the bizarre behaviors including the psychological symptoms and physical actions of these soldiers did appear to have little to do with the actions of an ailing heart. It was clearly the brain that had been damaged, shocked by the close proximity to the ongoing and unrelenting barrages of exploding shells that had become so much a part of the new kind of static trench warfare.

If you came out of a battle or bombardment unwounded but sweating, disoriented, paralyzed, or simply unable to go on, you were diagnosed as having been too close to the shelling. The symptoms of depression and anxiety, the agitation and confusion, were viewed as the results of neurological damage caused by both the noise and commotion of the high-energy explosions.

The physicians of the time, trained and experienced in the organically oriented institutionalized psychiatry of the late nineteenth and early twentieth centuries, agreed among themselves that clearly these visibly shaken men truly had something physically wrong with their brains—not their minds, their brains. The medical judgment as well as diagnosis was that the concussions from the exploding shells must have surely, and in some real but unknown way, rattled the tissues of these poor troopers' central nervous systems.

Despite hundreds of fortuitous autopsies that showed no evidence at all of significant brain damage, and the occasional afflicted soldier who had never even been near an exploding shell, physicians persisted in giving these troopers a diagnosis of "Shell Shock," and for the worst of them, the implication of irreversible brain damage.

It was of course a handy theory. If the shell-shocked patient recovered completely, the concussion had not been severe. If the soldier did not fully recover, the damage was considered to be more extensive, and then if the patient never improved, irreversible. If the patient intermittently lapsed back into bizarre or depressive behaviors, the damage was said to lie somewhere between these two extremes.

A diagnosis of shell shock was not only medically convenient, it was both militarily and politically correct. The theory of tumult and commotion damaging the brain became an excuse that was both accessible and acceptable to everyone. Family, friends, and the nation were now able to think of their loved ones as victims as well as heroes. After all, it was the shells that did it. To admit otherwise would have meant the son, the father, the lover, and the country had all failed. The problem, though, of trying to squeeze observable facts into an acceptable but inappropriate theory is that it never works. Sooner or later, the truth comes out. Still, it was as difficult to admit to the crippling effects of the battlefield during the Civil War and World War I as it is now.

Like all of medicine, psychiatry, along with theories of mental illness, developed and progressed throughout the 1920s and '30s. Faced with these new understandings of psychology, less fashionable ideas about battlefield stress were proposed, though there remained the desire to maintain a completely physical version for those soldiers' refusal to go on or to once again put themselves in harm's way. Still for another sixty years, the physical won out, even though symptoms occurred in soldiers who had not survived sustained combat.

In World War II, the symptoms of "Shell Shock" simply morphed into "Battle Fatigue." Fear and anxiety were simply the result of physical exhaustion, of having been out in the field too long. A little rest, a little R & R, and all would be fine again. This idea of "Battle Fatigue" was carried forward into Korea as "Combat Exhaustion."

The psychology of the time had eliminated the need for the commotion of exploding shells. It was all exhaustion now and having to do a difficult job. There was nothing ominous or mysterious going on. Once again, exhaustion was something that was understandable and acceptable to those afflicted, to the culture, and to society in general. The stress of war was nothing more than being tired, of simply having had too much. Everyone could relate to that.

But the successes of Freud and the psychoanalytical movement during the 1930s and '40s had their effect on both psychiatry and the battlefield. The diagnosis of "Combat Neurosis" began to creep into the military vocabulary. There were now concerns about personality disorders, deep-seated anxieties, and unresolved childhood conflicts.

The conviction grew that there was something more complicated going on here than mere exhaustion. It was believed that, although rest was important, the routine short-term evacuation of these patients from the front was not part of the cure but part of the disease. Guilt at evacuation, of not doing one's duty, of leaving friends and colleagues to fight on alone, was felt to play a major part in both establishing and fixing symptoms.

Surviving while others died was thought to turn a few minutes of doubt and panic into lifelong disabilities. It was considered best to treat these soldiers as far forward on the battlefield as possible; that unit identification were best maintained; and that above all else, treatment was always to include the unwavering expectation, no matter how apparently tragic or disabling the symptoms, that these troopers would be returned to duty as soon as possible. The emphasis was to be placed on the previous health of the patient and not on the symptoms, on the soldier's ability to ultimately cope, and where necessary even on an official acknowledgment that for everyone the battlefield is indeed a terrible place. There was the mind to be considered now, as well as the brain.

By the time troops began moving into Vietnam, the use of tranquilizers had become available. The basic treatment for battlefield depression, hysteria, and anxiety became the use of large dosages of the newly available psychopharmological agent Thorazine. The idea was to drug these troopers in order to force them to rest, to let them sleep off their problems and then gradually allow them wake up, take a deep breath, and go back to their units.

Everyone quickly learned the drill. A trooper in the Ninth Division fighting in the Mekong Delta, or a Marine along the Demilitarized Zone, might panic, get himself wounded, or wound himself. He might even go to the chaplain or decide on the relative safety of the stockade. A soldier fighting in the Central Highlands or along the Cambodian border might develop psychosomatic complaints, grow angry, or become totally disoriented. A trooper of the First Air Cavalry on a sweep through Khe Sanh might become hostile, begin to shake, refuse to move, or go completely hysterical. A tanker of the Twenty-fifth Division might turn grossly psychotic: hold imaginary rifles, see dead comrades on every mede-vac chopper, or hear disembodied voices. No matter what, the treatment was always Thorazine, rest, and being sent back to the unit. Even those who didn't respond and after a second or third trial of Thorazine had to be medevaced to the hospitals in Da Nang or Saigon had their unit decals placed on their bedposts. Whatever else might be going on, these patients were still members of their units with the expectation that sooner, rather than later, they would all be going back to active duty.

For the most part, it worked. At least the Army thought so. In the more resistant cases, soldiers who couldn't rest even after their drug-induced sleep, whose functioning remained impaired, or those who were truly disoriented or had simply stopped func-tioning were sent on to the military hospitals in

Japan, Okinawa, and the Philippines, and, if necessary, from there to the States. But those troopers removed from combat were a decidedly small percentage of the large number of soldiers treated.

The point was that during the Vietnam War, the majority of patients with a psychiatric diagnosis did go back to duty. During the whole of the war, 100 percent of soldiers with an initial diagnosis of "Combat Exhaustion," 90 percent of the primary "Combat Neurosis," 98 percent of the alcoholic and drug problems, 56 percent of the supposed psychotics, and 85 percent of the psychoneurotics went back to their units with a bland, final nonjudgmental impression or diagnosis on their record of "Acute Situation Reaction." No ominous-sounding terms to disturb these patients, their units, their families or the country.

And of course, the military got what they wanted. The vast majority of soldiers were not lost to the fight. But they were also not lost to the terrifying nature of warfare and that crippling moment of hesitation that could become fixed forever in both time and place. But there were no follow-ups on these troopers after they were returned to duty. No one knew if they were the ones who died in the very next firefight; who, distracted or confused, called in the wrong artillery coordinates or missed the trip wire stretched out across the path. No one ever checked to see if these were the soldiers whose weapons jammed or went on to gun down unarmed civilians.

Apparently, the Army didn't want to know, and so no one checked.

But pain is pain. The mental health aspects of the battlefield are not so easily treated or easily dismissed. Once the Genie of the Mind is out of the bottle, there is no easy way of putting it back. Agitation, depression, guilt, mistrust, anger, and thoughts of suicide, as well as emotional anesthesia, along with the personal and social dysfunctions, are complicated affairs and can be as devastating as the loss of any limb and as permanent as any penetrating head wound. Large dosages of Thorazine, a little rest, and a unit decal on a hospital bed in a battalion aid station are not enough.

During the 1970s—when veterans of the Vietnam War began to flood the VA hospitals, demanding that something be done to alleviate their anguish and despair—the emotional aspects of the battlefield were finally studied in a rigorous way. By 1980, these patients were being given a new diagnosis that better defined their psychological symptoms: PTSD, or Post-Traumatic Stress Disorder.

The use of the term PTSD put both the cause and treatment of psychiatric battlefield trauma on a solid research and therapeutic basis. No more nonsense; no more pseudoscience or self-serving obfuscations. It was as if the germ theory had finally come to the study of infectious diseases.

The Army's goal has always been to keep its troops in line and, where necessary, at the tip of the spear. It had always been easier for the military to blame the psychiatric problems of being in battle on the disruptive physical forces at work rather than on the apparent vagueness of fear, mental confusion, and emotional trauma. That's all far too touchy-feely for the military. After all, everyone in a firefight, indeed anyone who has ever stepped into a jeep or, in the Iraq War, into a Humvee, runs the risk of dying, of becoming wounded, or of seeing others being killed—often for no other apparent reason than being in the wrong place at the wrong time. Just being in a war and the sheer happenstance of it all are terrifying. No one ever denied that much about combat. But not everyone breaks down or gives up. There is and has always been real value to that "band of brothers" camaraderie among soldiers, to the growth in maturity and self-awareness that occur in surviving a terrible experience, as well the understandings and sympathy that come from making it through a difficult time. There remained both within the military and the public a sense of clarity and correctness, as documented in the 1970 movie *Patton*. George C. Scott, playing General George S. Patton, slaps a "yellow-bellied soldier" on a visit to a military hospital as both a reprimand and the treatment for the supposed cowardice. That is the way we would like it to be, that is the way the Army would like it, but that is not the way it is. We are, despite our own misgivings, not so much thinking animals who feel as feeling animals who think.

PTSD is real. It begins on the battlefield and can be as disabling as an amputated leg or a transected spinal cord. The medical path to the diagnosis began in 1947 in a paper by Kardiner and Spiegel, "War Stress and Neurotic Illness," which described a persistent chronic and disabling war-induced neurosis consisting of nightmares, irritability, and a tendency toward angry outbursts, along with a general impairment of overall functioning.

Half a dozen years later an article was published in *The American Journal of Psychiatry* reporting the prevalence and persistence of what at the time was still called "Traumatic War Neurosis" in a study of two hundred psychiatric patients who became symptomatic during and following the World War II. Physicians involved in the study continued to observe significant symptoms in these war veterans up to ten years after the end of combat.

A fifteen-year follow-up of these same World War II veterans, along with Korean War servicemen, continued to document severe and persistent problems including startled reactions, significant sleep disturbances, and the avoidance of activities even slightly reminiscent of combat. The Korean War veterans showed the same initial psychological profile as the World War II servicemen, with an increase in both the number and severity of symptoms in combat controls compared with the noncombatant veterans.

But the acceptance of post-traumatic stress disorder as an authentic and reliable psychological diagnosis has been an uphill fight, even though it is an ecumenical disease, not restricted to any war or to any specific group of soldiers.

Symptoms and percentages of PTSD among Israeli soldiers who fought in the 1982 Lebanon war proved similar to those of U.S. troops in Vietnam, Mogadishu, and now Afghanistan and Iraq. PTSD is now considered to be a long-term and in many cases—particularly if undiagnosed, untreated, or undertreated—persistent and crippling reaction to the stress of battle.

It is true that preexisting psychiatric conditions, such as depression, antisocial personality, alcohol and substance abuse, can be associated with a diagnosis of PTSD. But a high incidence of war-zone as well as battlefield exposures dramatically increases the risk of developing the condition.

A survey of American soldiers deployed to Somalia supports this view. When the original mission of the U.S. troops in Mogadishu shifted through mission creep from humanitarian peacekeeping to the more familiar battlefield assignment of subduing a Somali warlord, there was an increase in the incidence of PTSD among those U.S. troops, with the greatest incidence in those exposed to both the physical dangers and the psychological trauma of actual warfare.

The importance of actual combat in the development of PTSD became even clearer in a 1995 study involving veterans of the Persian Gulf War. Deaths and combat casualties were blissfully light, but the prevalence rate for PTSD was 10.1 percent among those who experienced actual combat, compared with 4.2 percent in a matched cohort of troopers who remained in support units.

It is expected that with the ever-increasing exposure to combat situations of all troops now in Iraq, there will be substantial increases in rates of PTSD similar to those seen in Somalia—especially as the campaign has shifted from a war of liberation to one of ongoing occupation involving increases in armed conflict with dissident combatants.

That fact is already becoming evident in the most recent evaluations. The exposure to combat is significantly higher among troops deployed to Iraq than those deployed to Afghanistan, and the incidence of PSTD among troops in Iraq has gone up substantially in relationship to similar units in Afghanistan.

An evaluation done by the Department of Psychiatry and Behavioral Services at the Walter Reed Army Institute of Research has continued to show what is becoming unarguable: "The percentage of study subjects whose responses met the screening criteria for major depression, generalized anxiety, or PTSD was significantly higher after duty in Iraq (15.6 to 17.1 percent) than after duty in Afghanistan (11.2 percent); while before deployment to Iraq the combined incidence was 9.3 percent. The greatest difference was in the rates of PTSD."

All military data up to the present time, every

meta-analysis of studies on wartime stress, collectively points out the critical issue of time on the battlefield as well as combat as preconditions for the development of PTSD. This fact has become more important to military mental health personnel, as the Iraq War has morphed into a guerrilla war where there are no front lines and where Reserve and National Guard troops are as likely to come under fire as the frontline combat units.

The point to all this is that every American unit can be involved in hazardous duty. The troops with the highest percentage of PSTD in the different surveys have always been those who were exposed to high levels of combat experiences. Even in the oldest studies, more than 90 percent of those diagnosed with post-traumatic stress disorder reported having been shot, attacked by enemy combatants, or involved in some kind of deadly firefight. In Iraq virtually everyone, whatever his or her status, supply or combat, regular Army, National Guard, or Reserve, has seen or had to deal with dead bodies, knows or has heard of someone who was injured or killed, or has himself or herself been attacked. The incidence of the disorder can only be expected to increase the longer these units are kept in country.

Charles W. Hoge, M.D., in his article "Combat Duty in Iraq and Afghanistan, Mental Health Problems, and Barriers to Care," reported a prevalence of PTSD of 12.7 percent among U.S. troops after they had been in three to five firefights, and of 19.3

percent after more than five. The author admits that these are conservative estimates that do not take into account those severely wounded.

Despite increasing rates of PTSD, the true incidence may still be underreported. A retrospective report on PTSD documented what most in the military already know: specifically, that of those whose evaluations were positive for a mental disorder, only 23 to 40 percent complained of or sought help for mental health problems while still on active duty.

There remains the widely held notion on the part of either active-duty personnel or those on career officer tracks, that anyone who seeks help or counseling, even when they or their colleagues clearly recognize the severity of their psychiatric problems, will be stigmatized and will jeopardize their own military careers. A recent survey of those returning from Iraq and Afghanistan indicated that those soldiers reporting the most severe symptoms were the least likely to seek treatment, for fear it would harm careers, cause difficulty with peers, and be an admission of weakness and, worse, of cowardice in the face of the enemy.

In the military culture, "succumbing" to PTSD continues to be seen as a failure, a weakness, and evidence of not having "the right stuff." It is a view that the present leaders in the Pentagon appear reluctant to challenge or to change.

No one knows whether those with PTSD who remain undiagnosed and so untreated, upon their return to civilian life, fail at reintegration, and become criminals or even murderers. Veterans who are diagnosed with PTSD do have more divorces, more marital problems, and more occupational instability, along with all the associated social dysfunctions, including higher levels of homelessness, more criminal arrests, and more acts of violence, than do veterans without a diagnosis of PTSD.

But there is more to not encouraging or seeking treatment than simply not wanting to deal with the problem. For soldiers and their families, there are real consequences to ignoring or postponing dealing with the stresses of war. Delayed forms of PTSD are now well documented. As late as 1993, a study of World War II Dutch resistance fighters indicated a subacute form of PTSD that had gradually become chronic, a delayed form with onset five to thirty-five years after the end of the conflict, and an intermittent subtype filled with decades of relapses and remissions. Israeli psychiatrists observed reactivation of PTSD among veterans of the 1967 Yom Kippur War when exposed to the war-zone stress of the 1982 Lebanon war.

Without diagnosis and treatment, the psychological stresses of war never really end. That so many troops and veterans of the Iraq War are complaining of psychiatric illness as well as PTSD symptoms compared with those troops and veterans of previous wars, may have as much to do with a change in the makeup of troops conducting the Iraq War as it does with a change in attitude on the part of psychiatrists in general and military psychology in particular. More than 40 percent of the American soldiers in Iraq are now Reservists or National Guard troops. They are older than the typical active-duty soldiers. Few, if any, are making the Army a career. Many on extended or second deployments have the additional stress of families to worry about and careers left on hold.

War is always more difficult for those who are older and have personal commitments and responsibilities that go beyond their units, their comrades, and even their own sense of patriotism.

No one who understands this war found it unusual or unexpected that it was an older Tennessee National Guardsman—not a nineteen-year-old Marine or a twenty-one-year-old corporal in the Third Armor Division—who stood up at a "meet with the troops visit" and publicly complained to Defense Secretary Donald H. Rumsfeld about the lack of adequately armored vehicles and the fact that he and his comrades had to search through scrap heaps to find armored plates to up-armor their own Humvees. It is always more difficult to sell snake oil to grown-ups.

The nasty little secret about this war's deployment is that the percentages of people whose responses meet the screening criteria for PTSD are highest among members of the National Guard and Reserve units, and that those screening results are clearly higher after deployments than before deployments. There is also a bit of irony here. The World War I physicians who offered up the diagnosis "shell shock" more out of a cultural desperation than medical science are proving partly correct in their original assessments of the physical shaking of the brain as a cause of psychiatric symptoms, even if their diagnosis had to wait nearly a hundred years to be accepted. Iraq and Afghanistan have finally brought together the brain and the mind. It is clear today that subtle TBIs can and do result in post-traumatic stress disorder and may be a major cause of this condition in those exposed to the blast effects of roadside bombs. The treatments, though, for the mind or the brain, remain the same.

The good news is that with the use of the newer antidepressant medications, along with group and individual therapy, PTSD can be treated and in some cases cured, while in the majority of other patients as with any other chronic psychiatric disorder, PTSD can be kept under control. But treatments cost money—and with the large number of patients involved, lots of money. Yet PTSD symptoms remain the most frequently reported problems noted in anonymous surveys among those soldiers returning from duty in Iraq and Afghanistan.

The statistics on the number of Iraqi civilians killed or wounded, even estimates, are notoriously absent from official documents as well as news dispatches or interviews from the front lines of the war.

There has been no administrative attempt to index or order the so-called collateral damage. Still, those deaths and injuries—particularly of women and children killed in the large sweeps through towns and villages and at roadblocks—have taken their own unique and unexpected psychological toll on the older U.S. troops, particularly those who are parents themselves. It is this group of Reservists and National Guard troops who experience flashbacks and late episodes of PTSD after being confronted with the mangled bodies of civilians caught in the cross hairs of insurgent or friendly fire.

"We were supposed to be in a secure area. Hell, we're a maintenance unit. We set up the roadblock. The sedan didn't stop. It looked like a lot of people in the backseat. Someone yelled, "Gun." You don't have a lot of time to decide. Fifty-caliber rounds can do an awful lot of damage to a Toyota. When we opened the back door, one of the guys started to throw up. There were three little girls in the back seat. Two were cut in half and the third was missing her head . . . "

The need for timely psychiatric interventions and ongoing psychological treatment has become particularly true for those tens of thousands who have been wounded. Patients with physical disabilities that are the result of war-zone injuries clearly have the highest rates of PTSD. This is something that has been known since the early 1980s. The wounded are particularly vulnerable to unremitting PTSD. Successful treatment is complicated because therapy must deal with the patient's physical as well as psychological problems. Moreover, among the severely wounded, sounds and events similar to those connected with the original injuries, if reexperienced even years later, can trigger all the original fears and anxieties. Reoccurrence of PTSD has been documented following experiences associated with later stressful life events such as aging and retirement. PTSD can be a disease without end.

During the most recent 2005 federal budget cycle, funding for the nation's Department of Veterans Affairs was increased less than 1 percent, while specific PTSD programs as well as inpatient psychiatric facilities and follow-up outpatient clinics have been cut back. Senior Veterans Administration officials have made the argument before Congress that in a time of large deficits with the needs for fiscal restraints, the VA currently has enough funds available to do what has to be done. An executive administration that cannot bring itself to up-armor its own army's vehicles or admit that it made an error in force structure can hardly be expected to address the mental health of those same troops. The *Wall Street Journal* in October of 2005, two years after our troops entered Iraq, finally got this part of the war right. In an article set above the fold entitled "I'm not the Same Person," the *Journal* documents what is happening to so many:

This summer, Nate Self's wife caught him staring at his old Army uniforms, hung neatly in his closet.

"What was all this for?" the 28-year-old former Army Ranger asked. His wife, Julie, tried to reassure him. "Nathan, you did great, great things in the Army," she recalls telling him.

In January 2003, the Army Ranger captain sat in the Capitol as the president's guest while Mr. Bush gave his State of Union address. To the White House, Mr. Self was a symbol of American strength, resolve and success in the war on terror. Badly outgunned, the young officer led his men through a bloody 15-hour firefight against al Qaeda fighters atop a remote mountain in Afghanistan.

After the battle, the Army awarded him the Silver Star, heaped praise on him and assumed he would move swiftly onto the next war. He did. In the spring of 2003, he deployed to Iraq. There, Mr. Self began to suffer from grisly nightmares, anxiety and depression.

Last year the war hero came home. In November, he quietly—and inexplicably, to his Army friends—left the military. A few months later, he was diagnosed with severe post-traumatic stress disorder.

Today, Mr. Self presents a different sort of model for the Army. He's a striking example of the emotional toll the wars in Iraq and Afghanistan are taking on soldiers and the U.S. government's incomplete efforts to respond. Just as the U.S. military underestimated many things in Iraq—the insurgency, the need for better body armor and stronger vehicles—it didn't anticipate the levels of emotional stress soldiers have faced.

Shakespeare said it best: "The abuse of greatness is when it disjoins remorse from power."

Oaths

"How the hell did all this happen?"

—WOUNDED MARINE,
TET OFFENSIVE, MARCH, 1968

There has been something a bit off about this war from the beginning, that went beyond the "bait and switch" from Afghanistan to Iraq, the lack of Weapons of Mass Destruction and the fact that there was no connection between the attack on the World Trade Center and Saddam Hussein.

It is that sense of the backyard bully, that "Bring 'em on" and "Bin Ladin Dead or Alive," that seemed unnecessary and worse, dangerous.

But still it is one thing to beat your chest and think you are the biggest kid on the block and quite another to go about trashing the rules that hold the neighborhood together. Efforts have been made throughout history to eliminate or, at least, control the excesses of warfare. The theories of the "Just

War," the Geneva Conventions, the Red Cross and Red Crescent Accords, and the Uniform Codes of Military Justice are all attempts to keep war from spilling over the edge. Despite what the uninitiated might say, out in the desperateness of the battlefield there is all the difference between the merciless and the pitiless.

There was a communication, perhaps apocryphal, but widely believed and discussed, between Robert E. Lee and President Abraham Lincoln at the beginning of the Civil War. A company of Federal cavalry, working as a detached unit, was captured by the Confederates, and the orders carried by the captain of the company sent on to Robert E. Lee.

The orders were as ruthless as they were specific. The cavalry was given carte blanche to wreak havoc throughout the South. Their orders were to burn, to maim, to pillage, and to kill. These orders were so clearly outside the accepted rules of engagement that Robert E. Lee sent them on to Lincoln with a note that asked basically, is this the kind of war you want? Lincoln answered no, that this was not the kind of war that he nor anyone else in the Union wanted, and he made that perfectly clear to his own Department of War.

Lincoln understood that even in war there were lines that should not be crossed. He realized that someday the nation would have to be put back together again and that how the war was fought would, in the end, be as important as how it was won.

This administration apparently holds no such view. Restraint is not part of its politics nor policy; the Geneva Conventions are said to no longer apply; the president is said to have unlimited powers to fight the "War on Terror"; tribunals are to replace civilian as well as military courts, the Patriot Act, memos from the highest levels of the Justice Department authorizing "harsh" interrogation techniques, the bellicose landing of a president on aircraft carriers, "Preventive War," Abu Ghraib, Guantánamo—the list goes on.

A military, though, is never comfortable with the dimming of legal distinctions and blurring of established and official boundaries. Vagueness in military orders inevitably means approval or consent. Whether captain, private, general, or ensign, anyone who has ever worn a uniform knows that much about being in the Armed Forces. If orders are vague, you are pretty much being told to do as you please or what you think your superiors want you to do. Still, as thin as these generally accepted rules might be, or as this administration would have it, however "outdated," those limitations and prohibitions on how wars are fought are put in place to protect both winners and losers alike.

Taken a step further, the loss of accepted standards in dealing with prisoners and detainees undermines the protections of our own troops. That is something the military understands, and that is why Colin Powell, the only Bush Cabinet official with combat experience, objected to the administration's memos authorizing a change in interrogation techniques of prisoners as well as the new classification of detainees. What is being talked about here is torture. In its zeal to accomplish its goal, this administration—as it has with virtually everything else with this war—is even willing to turn medicine on its head.

David Tornberg, the current Deputy Assistant Secretary of Defense for Health Affairs, a representative and spokesman on military medical policy for the Bush presidency, has publicly endorsed a Pentagon decision that physicians serving in interrogations of detainees are not acting as physicians. The Pentagon and the administration simply contend that physicians assigned to military intelligence have no doctor-patient relationship with the detainees and, in the absence of any life-threatening emergency, have no obligation to offer medical aid or be involved with what they call "old-fashioned" professional or ethical concerns.

Tornberg, a physician himself, appointed by Secretary of Defense Rumsfeld to the position of Deputy Assistant Secretary for Health Affairs, in an interview published in the *New England Journal of Medicine*, maintained that, in the absence of life-threatening emergencies, it is both professional, reasonable and expected for military physicians to participate in interrogation procedures, assist in the design, if not the implementation of interrogation strategies and where necessary to tailor coercive measures to a detainee's specific medical conditions.

Brazen, to say the least, and nonsense at best. Few ethicists, fewer physicians, and probably even fewer laypeople would agree with the Bush administration's assessment that a medical degree is not a "sacramental vow." But that is precisely what it is and has been since the time of Hippocrates, and no amount of political spin nor partisan fervor is going to change that.

The Hippocratic oath and all that it means is quite clear and, indeed, unequivocal: "Whatever houses I may visit, I will come for the benefit of the sick, remaining free of all intentional injustice. . . . "

Whatever excuses the Bush administration might give in turning its military physicians into company hacks and abusers, the most frequent is as follows, as expressed in an '04 Pentagon memo: "When a physician participates in an interrogation, he is not functioning as a physician and the Hippocratic ethic of commitment to a patient's welfare does not apply." Spin is one thing; blind arrogance is quite another.

That physicians who serve the country as military officers might not, in certain cases, be acting as physicians is lunacy. Physicians are chosen by the Pentagon to perform medical tasks, whatever those tasks, specifically and uniquely, because those officers are physicians.

Physicians are asked to participate in interrogations because they are physicians and have those unique medical skills that the Pentagon believes necessary to perform a successful inquiry. During interrogations, military physicians are asked to use their medical knowledge, their clinical skills as healers, and their knowledge of drugs, as well as their psychiatric insights as mental health professionals. Once a doctor, always a doctor—and that is a truth—whether this government wants to change the rules or whether or not they are willing to admit that basic fact of medical training and the medical ethos.

What is so troubling is that there have been those in the military who either agree with this administration's position or are reluctant to challenge their bosses. In interviews, physicians who have been and are willing to talk about their involvement do not see what they did as unethical. Indeed, these physicians bought the view that in helping to plan interrogations and aid the interrogators, they were not serving in the role of a physician and therefore are not bound by patient-oriented ethics.

Other military physicians who cared for so-called high-valued detainees have been especially hesitant to share their observations. Others who have spent time in detention facilities in Iraq and Guantánamo have been told not to talk about their experiences or give their impressions of what they saw. In the Army, it is a difficult and at times a dangerous task to disagree with a commanding officer, or not to do what you are ordered or expected to do. In Vietnam, physicians who disagreed or openly opposed their commanders were sent to frontline Battalion Aid Stations or ordered to go out on patrols with combat units. In the military, those in charge not only have their say, they get their way. As so often happens with the decisions of the Bush administration there is more at stake here than simply forcing physicians to no longer be physicians. The old rules, specifically the Geneva Conventions, protect medical personnel who serve in noncombatant roles—whether physicians, physician assistants, nurses, or medics—from direct attack. But there is a price to be paid for this protection. Medical professionals are bound by the same conventions, as well as by other international laws, to treat wounded combatants from all sides and to care for injured civilians. Trashing the values embodied in the Hippocratic oath for some marginal and at best suspicious gain is to undermine what has given medicine its prestige and power. The true value of medicine, its intrinsic virtue and its respect throughout history, has had little to do with its therapeutic mission, but with its commitment and responsibility to the individual to the exclusion of all other considerations. Physicians are to be healers, not participants. To ignore that prohibition is to blur the role of healer and put at risk the whole system of wartime care and the protection of medical personnel, whether ours or theirs.

It is dangerous to tinker, even about the edges, with the real and cross-cultural sense that medicine is, both as a personal as well as a healing art, a profession with no perceived interest other than to the patient and certainly no responsibility or duty to any third party—any third party... whether a relative, an employer, an insurer, or the state.

In October 2005, the Senate passed a bill, with an overwhelming majority of ninety-nine Senators to one, ensuring appropriate care of prisoners and detainees in the Bush Administration's fight against terrorism. The bill, opposed by the Bush Administration, to eliminate the use of torture was introduced by those few in the Senate, Republican and Democrat alike, who have been in the military and in actual combat. They understand. Despite the Presidential threat of a veto, the bill passed; but with the President reserving the right under the rather vague war powers of the Executive to ignore, if necessary, the law in the ongoing War on Terror.

As a society, we have already decided on how we want our doctors to both act and behave. We do not believe that physicians should administer the death penalty, even though in our country, capital punishment is lawful; nor do we feel comfortable when physicians perform abortions or consider taking a patient off life support. Physicians should be physicians. That is the way it has always been; the way it should be; it is the way *we* want it, and the way it has to be. It is what the physicians at Walter Reed in Washington, DC, and at Brooks Army Medical Center, want. It is what those at the Twenty-fourth Combat Surgical Hospital in Baghdad want. And it is what the surgeons out in the desert along the Syrian border want. One would think it is something our government would want.

A Matter of Class

"There is no one with a lawn service who knows or writes to anyone in Iraq or Afghanistan."

—CONVERSATION, ORTHOPEDIC SURGEON,
THIRD ARMORED CALVARY

As a nation, we have never endorsed the idea of a large, freestanding volunteer army. The Revolutionary War has been our model. It is the Citizen Army we turn to in times of danger. We have always been uncomfortable with the potential mischief that can result from an army separated from its people. Common sense has led us to believe that in times of actual confrontation and conflict, a standing army would never offer up enough "boots on the ground" to win our battles, much less go on to win our wars.

But we are not fools and do have a professional officer corps. In the more than two hundred years since the founding of the United States Military Academy at West Point, we have had a number of national debates about the wisdom of supporting a military elite, dedi-

115

cated to the arts of war, as well as the expected "Duty, Honor, Country." The argument was settled in favor of an officer corps in the late 1840s, following the successful West Point–led Mexican War of 1847–48. The purse strings, though, as well as the decisions of war and peace, have remained solidly in the hands of our elected officials.

But in a democracy, that old adage that "war is too important to be left to the generals" can become a two-edged sword. Politicians can be as foolish as any general and, faced with a population that is not involved or doesn't care all that much about what is happening, can cause as much damage to a nation as any jingoistic field marshal. Add to the mix a volunteer army, removed from an unconcerned or uninformed electorate, pushed on by an imperious government, and you have the ingredients for disaster—specifically, the implementing of narrow, self-serving decisions leading to ever-more-widening and unexpected consequences.

It was the growing lack of public support, as the war in Vietnam began escalating out of control, that forced General Creighton Abrams, who replaced General William Westmoreland in 1968 as Commander of U.S. troops in Vietnam, to rethink the whole issue of public war and private commitment.

General Abrams came to view Vietnam as a war being fought by an army cut off from the population it served. What Abrams saw was that by late 1969 the majority of combat units in Vietnam were made up of blacks from Cleveland, Detroit, and Philadelphia,

Hispanics from Texas and California, and poor Southern whites. Abrams understood the inequity in all this and realized that this kind of smoldering demographic, barely working in a country at peace, would never work in a country involved in a deadly war going badly.

He became convinced that it was the separation of those who serve from those being served that had opened up the country to divisiveness and the military to a conflict that had not been well thought out and so was ultimately doomed to failure. General Abrams was well aware that the Vietnam draft had skewed conscription to the poor and disfranchised and away from those in positions of power, prestige, wealth, and privilege. The pain and suffering were simply not being shared between the risk takers and those who had put the country at risk. Abrams was aware of the long history of inequities in conscription, going back to the Civil War and Congress's 1863 legislation that allowed draftees to hire substitutes, paying a $300 fee to avoid the whole conscription process.

There had been nothing as egregious nor as flagrant as a $300 exception during the Vietnam War, but in a more sophisticated way, those kind of exemptions did exist. By 1968 there was no end to the numbers and types of military deferments. There were undergraduate deferments for college and graduate school deferments. There were deferments for enlistment in the National Guard and Reserve units, there were medical deferments if you were connected enough to have a specialist document that you did have a certain degree of scoliosis that did, or might or would lead to, back pain under the stress and strain of military duty, not to mention flat feet and severe nearsightedness.

But the single most egregious example of protecting the privileged from the risks of going to war was the decision by Robert S. McNamara, the Secretary of Defense under President Lyndon B. Johnson and one of the architects of our involvement in Vietnam, to lower the IQ standards of potential draftees. This led to an additional 100,000 troops with borderline intelligence going off, each year from 1965 to 1968, to fight for their country. These soldiers were called—with both sympathy and derision by those who had to train and then watch over them and then fight with them—"McNamara's 100,000."

In a response to this "privilege gap" and to make sure that it never happened again, Abrams recommended that the regular Army be kept small and that if, in the future, any substantial large-scale military action be considered, that the National Guard and Reserve units be called up, giving all Americans a quick, abiding, and immediate interest in any administration's opting for a major military option, much less going to war. The idea was simple enough; for anything more than a police action, the citizens of the country would be forced to become engaged through the activation and overseas deployment of their own state's National Guard and Reserve units.

General Abrams, who had served in World War II,

was sure that if the cause was right, a generalized civil commitment—whatever the casualties—would be possible again. You do have to believe in the government's position, or at least in a greater good, to put your own body or the body of a family member, friend, local police officer, or neighborhood fireman in harm's way. Without the equal sharing of risks and dangers, what is offered up as national priorities, much less as national security, is quickly abandoned. In short, in times of war, if you don't go or someone you care about or know doesn't go, than someone goes in your place. Eventually embarrassment on the part of those who stay home and anger on the part of those who go unhinge the balance of things.

And that is today's situation. It was the country at war that General Abrams hoped to address by keeping any future army small, relying, if necessary, on the National Guard and Reservists initially to fight any new wars, forcing a reluctant or uninvolved populous to become concerned, or at least be part of the discussion.

Eventually Abrams's fear that Vietnam would be lost came true. But others saw the military itself as being derelict in its duty to the country. Colonel Harry G. Summers in his *On Strategy: A Critical Analysis of the Vietnam War*, puts the military responsibility for the failure of Vietnam in terms that ring true today.

> ... throughout the 1960s the military were torn between the commitment to

civilian supremacy inculcated through generations of service and their premonition of
disaster, between trying to make a new system work and rebelling against it. They
were demoralized by the order to procure
weapons in which they did not believe and
by the necessity of fighting a war whose
purpose proved to be increasingly elusive.
A new breed of military officer emerged:
men who learned the new jargon, who
could present the systems analysis argu-
ments so much in vogue, more articulate
than the older generations and more skilled
in bureaucratic maneuvering. On some levels it eased civilian-military relationships;
on a deeper level, it deprived the policy
process of the simpler, cruder, but perhaps
more relevant assessments which in the
final analysis are needed when issues are
reduced to a test of arms . . .

National bewilderment at our failure in Vietnam
along with contempt and disgust for anything military
led to the development of an all-volunteer army in the
1970s and 1980s simply to keep a military in place and
the wheels turning. Out of necessity, General Abrams
was eventually to get his wish of that smaller regular
army backed by Reserve units. Abrams died in 1974,
after serving as Chief of Staff of the United States
Army as the military began its transition to an all-

volunteer force. The results of that transition, though, were not as General Abrams had hoped or expected. Twenty-five years after the collapse in Vietnam, we did again have a confident, self-assured and professional military that took on and beat Saddam Hussein's Republican Guards in less than a hundred hours during the first Persian Gulf War.

During the 1980s, the Army trained officers like H. R. McMaster, currently the colonel leading the Third Armored Cavalry Regiment in Iraq. In 1991, during the Persian Gulf War, McMaster, a West Point graduate, was a captain leading the 10 M1 Abrams tanks and 13 Bradley Fighting Vehicles of Eagle Troop of the 2nd Armored Cavalry Regiment in the breakout through Kuwait. During the first hours of the war, McMaster took on what amounted to a Republican Guard Regiment of T-72 tanks, destroying over 20 Iraqi tanks along with a large number of other armored vehicles without any US casualties. When asked how he felt confronting dozens of T-72 Russian heavy tanks with less than a quarter that number of his own tanks, he answered without the slightest hesitation or hint of the professional confusion that had been so much a part of our military in Vietnam, "I was surprised at how much more accurate the live ammunition was than the dummy rounds we had been training with in Germany." New Army, new attitude, new weapon systems, new successes. At the end of the Persian Gulf War, both the country and the military took a deep, comfortable breath and relaxed.

But a standing army costs money. Economics both in war and in peace does come into play. By the end of the end of the 1990s, the military had been shrunk from the 4 million of the Vietnam War era to a total of a little less than 1.4 million. The Army was meeting its monthly voluntary recruitment goals, and America, having forged a professional, talented, and dedicated military were told that we could, with the volunteer force at hand, win two wars fought simultaneously.

General Abrams has been given his wish, or part of it. He had that smaller, more nimble, yet power-ful volunteer force. What he had not expected nor anticipated was a major war where the Pentagon would be forced to call up National Guard and Reservist units to fill out the need for additional troops, but where the country, indifferent to their neighbors' being called up to fill in as combat troops, would do and say nothing. He had not envi-sioned a country that would send off Reserve and National Guard troops without becoming engaged nor demand an accounting of wartime policy, goals, and purposes. What would have surprised Abrams was that so few cared.

In a very real way, General Abrams might well have gotten the worst of both worlds. The Army has recruited its enlisted ranks almost exclusively from that portion of the population in which the military is viewed, if not as a way out, then certainly as a way up. That Vietnam divide between those who serve and those who are served has become the foundation of the volunteer force; out of necessity National Guard and Reserve units now account for more than 40 percent of the active-duty troops fighting in Iraq and Afghanistan. All with little public complaint or outcry and even less political comment.

And the numbers and sacrifice are staggering. In August 2005, the 408th Minnesota Air National Guard Fighter Wing, with more than four hundred airmen, was sent to Iraq. Some of the airmen were rotating back for a second and third time.

Before the end of the year, an additional 2,700 Minnesota National Guard were sent to Iraq in the largest single deployment of Minnesota Guard troops since World War II. It is not that we don't know these troops or who they are. Newspaper photographs and twenty-second spots on the evening news has made that perfectly clear. For the most part, these are middle-aged men and single mothers. The men are overweight and clearly out of shape and the women look exhausted, the distress clearly etched into their faces as they hold their kids to say good-bye. These are in reality part-time soldiers, who now have to worry about mortgages, car payments, dental bills, gas, hair cuts, new clothes, who will go to the kids' sports events, birthdays and the confusion over who will be responsible for maintaining health-care benefits while they are away from their jobs for the twelve to eighteen months of their deployments—and all this while they are running the most dangerous roads in the world.

But this war is not only stretching the military, it is stretching the country. State governors, meeting at the National Governor's Conference in Des Moines, Iowa, during the summer of 2005, were overtly critical of the burden these National Guard deployments have placed on their states' ability to cope with their own emergencies, natural or man-made. The governors were clearly worried that the deployment of their states' Guard units to Iraq leaves their states unprotected against floods and other natural disasters while creating gaps in the numbers of "First Responders," including health-care and law-enforcement personnel. The governors of Idaho and Montana expressed concerns that without the Guard units, their states would not be able to cope with the expected forest fires sure to occur over the approaching summer months.

These domestic fears became reality when Hurricane Katrina struck New Orleans and the levees protecting the city burst. As security failed, three hundred National Guard soldiers from Wisconsin along with Guard units from other states were mobilized for duty in Louisiana. Whatever the reasons given for calling up the National Guard from states as far as a thousand miles from the disaster, there were few in those units who did not believe they were being sent south because many of the Louisiana Guard units—along with much of their high-water equipment—were in Baghdad. National Guard troops who should and could have been on the streets of New Orleans and Gulf Point in hours took days to arrive. Americans viewing the devastation and lack of an immediate response suddenly realized both individually and as a country that the war had affected all of us and that as a nation we had been lulled into a kind of sleepwalking trance.

It is part of this national anesthesia that out of a country of almost 300 million people, we have allowed fewer than 135,000 at any one time, including rotations and additional deployments of some 130,000 women to take on the whole burden of fighting a war. In the week Katrina came ashore, fourteen Marines form the Third Battalion 25th Marines, a Reserve unit from Brook Park, Ohio, were killed when their amphibious troop carrier was torn apart by an enormous bomb. The lightly armored amphibious personnel carriers were designed in the 1960s to bring Marines ashore during amphibious operations. They were only to be used within a half mile of the landing beaches and were not designed to transport Marines through enemy towns or along dangerous desert highways. The Marines who were killed were clearly not properly equipped for the tasks at hand and paid the price for lack of both appropriate transport and adequate protection. Amphibious vehicles in a desert, lack of up-armored vehicles, and inadequate body armor should have been enough of a wake-up call that despite the pronouncements of success and the need to "stay the course," all is not going well. But the military reality is that there have never been enough troops on the ground.

Even in the race to Baghdad, at the very start of the war, when the Marines of the First Marine Division covered six hundred miles with dozens of firefights, winning every battle, from the borders of Kuwait up through Nasiariyah to the very outskirts of Baghdad, stopping only for a sandstorm that caused zero visibility for three days, that lack of adequate numbers of troops was noticed. In the midst of that effort, more than one Marine commented that, after they had left a liberated village or town, they could hear gunfire as their tanks, Humvees and Light Armored Vehicles or LAVs pulled away. "We didn't have enough troops to leave behind to really secure the towns or supply routes. Our job was just to keep going."

Two years later, units of the Kentucky National Guard killed fifty-six insurgents in a desperate three-hour firefight that one officer described as a well-organized attack by what amounted to three platoons of insurgents. National Guard troops should not routinely be put in dangerous situations where they are forced to hold their own in firefights simply to keep from being overrun.

Major General William G. Webster, commander of the Third Infantry Division, recently gave a rundown of troops available to meet the increase in suicide bombings, buried roadside bombs, and ambushes in the area under the Third's control. He has 27,000 American troops, 15,000 Iraqi policemen, and 7,000 Iraqi soldiers to control an area in which Saddam

Hussein routinely garrisoned some 80,000 troops and 50,000 police to ensure security.

Like those General Officers on the ground in Vietnam, General Webster would not or could not say the obvious, that he doesn't have enough troops. But this administration and this Pentagon knew that from the very beginning of Iraqi Freedom. It was General Eric K. Shinseki, the Chief of Staff of the Army, who warned Donald Rumsfeld, a month into the war, that the force structure allocated to Iraq would not be adequate. General Shinseki believed that a commitment of between 250,000 and 300,000 troops would be necessary, not so much to win the war, but to hold the peace. General Shinseki was ridiculed publicly by Rumsfeld, his assessment trashed by the spin doctors of the administration. Soon after his testimony, the general was forced to retire. The word was out; don't disagree with this administration if you want to remain in the military.

It is not so much that General Shinseki was right and that the lack of an adequate number of troops would plague the military up until the present time, but that months into the occupation, both the White House and the Pentagon ignored their own appointee to run the provisional civilian government. Paul Bremer, an effective and distinguished government official whose credentials as a diplomat go back to the time of Henry Kissinger, wrote in his book *My Year in Iraq* and explained on more than one television interview that, during a summer 2003 meeting with the General

Abizaid, Commander of Coalition Forces in Iraq, the general in replying to a question about adequate troop strength, did admit that having two more divisions or another 40,000 troops would make securing Baghdad a great deal easier. Bremer sent a message suggesting the need for more troops to both the White House and the Pentagon. He never received an answer.

In a way, historians will tell you that none of this is really new. Differences of opinion, both civil and military, occur in every war. What is different is that this war is being fought without any sense or pretense of communal sacrifice. This is, in fact, the first war fought at the same time that the government has cut taxes. Social and economic class in America has never been a comfortable thing to talk about in private, much less to discuss in public. It is the true third rail not only of politics, but of any discussion of American culture. In this war, as in Southeast Asia, privilege spells the difference between living and dying, between being crippled or blind for the rest of your life. Today once again, survival is a matter of class.

For decades, economists have talked about the growing disparities between the rich and the poor in this country, the gentrification of American cities into the haves and the have-nots, the crumbling of the middle class, and the growing gap between those with position, power, wealth, and prestige and those without.

It is just this issue of class that Josiah Bunting III, a veteran, a novelist, an author, and current president of the Harry Frank Guggenheim Foundation, addressed in his 2005 article "Class Warfare," published in *The American Scholar*. Bunting laments the loss of any sense of national duty and service that has been swept aside by wealth and privilege. He is angry and unabashedly direct in his criticism of the nation's new elite. "The business of war has become increasingly remote from a particular segment (the wealthy and the privileged) of the American people."

Bunting takes the issue of class further up the social ladder than most have been willing to go. "The war in Iraq . . . like Korea and Vietnam . . . has splintered away from the conscious concern of most of those in whose behalf it is said to be prosecuted." He points out that of the 2,000 killed, few of the dead are the children of those who lead this country, who control its resources and institutions, dictate its tastes and opinions, are blessed most abundantly with the country's bounty, or feed most lavishly upon its expensive entertainments and its treasures.

He points out the record of one of this country's most prestigious but unnamed boarding schools. During World War I, 40 of its 400 students served in the military; during World War II the number was 60; 10 during the Korean Conflict; 5 for the ten years of the Vietnam War; and, so far, none in Iraq and Afghanistan. The 1956 Princeton graduating class sent a little less than half of its 900 graduates into the military, some as volunteers, some drafted within two years of graduation. In 2004, that same university sent 9 out of a class of 1,100. Today's Marines, patrolling the streets of Fallujah, have the same attitudes, abilities, courage, and esprit de corps as the Marines of World War II, but today those prep school boys and college kids are missing. Bunting makes clear that the abandonment of a Citizen Army has only added to the national anesthesia concerning this war. None of which is good for the country, the military, or our democracy.

Bunting ends his article with a statement written by George Washington at the end of his presidency:

> It may be laid down as a primary position, and the basis of our system, that every Citizen who enjoys the protection of a free Government, owes not only a proportion of his property, but even of his personal service to the defense of it.

Bunting, General Abrams, and George Washington may yet get back that Citizen Army. It is doubtful that George W. Bush or his administration will admit that their grand strategy to rid the world of evil and bring American democracy to the Middle East is coming apart and that what they are forcing on the military is now entering the realm of madness. But those in the military understand, whatever else this government might want or say, that this is not a nation at war, but only a military at war.

Barry McCaffrey, a retired four star general,

recently warned Congress that at the current rates of deployment, the country's National Guard will melt down sometime within the next twelve months. Regular Army units are being stretched thin, equipment is being run into the ground, troopers are fighting around the clock for days if not weeks on end, and there are not enough military personnel to do the job, much less protect what is there. Indeed, it looks as if the volunteer army that this government has pushed to its limits is itself running out of steam.

For the first time in the thirty-two-year existence of the all-volunteer force, our military is not reaching its monthly recruitment goals. This year, the Army will come up 80,000 new recruits short of the minimum needed to keep going at current force levels. Reenlistment in the National Guard is down some 40 percent; Reservist units are decreasing at half that rate. Whatever else can be said about this war, the country is clearly voting with its feet. The Chairman of the Joint Chiefs of Staff recently admitted that with our growing commitment in Iraq and Afghanistan, that fighting a second major war would most certainly result in a greater numbers of casualties than previously projected, and that victory, while ultimately assured, would take much longer to accomplish.

So this administration, instead of going up in society, has pushed enlistments further down the social ladder. The Army is currently lowering its induction standards, recruiting candidates barely meeting the lowest levels of military aptitude and the minimal IQ requirements. As one recruiter commented, "They are getting more GEDs in place of high school graduates . . . paying bonuses to people who wouldn't have qualified for a bonus before." It is, in many ways, Robert McNamara's 100,000 all over again, only worse because this time everyone knows what is happening and that includes the military.

But that isn't the end of it. The army plans to double its $20,000 enlistment bonus for "trigger-pullers" to $40,000. And if the young enlistees agree to be sent to one of the divisions bound for Iraq or Afghanistan in the next rotation, they will receive an extra pay raise of $400 a month for 36 months. As reprehensible as it is expected, this administration with its belief in capitalism and the marketplace has clearly decided that the best way to attract the youth of America to defend and protect both itself and us is to buy them.

There are, however, a growing number of field and general grade officers who will not let their military be trashed or debased. With Vietnam clearly in the rearview mirror, there are officers unwilling to fall on their swords for strategies and policies that have no merit and are ultimately dangerous and destructive to both the country and the military; officers who do not intend to go forward with this war or the next without the tools and numbers they need not only to win but to survive. Patriotism and love of country has never demanded constant sacrifice and blind obedience. That, too, is a legacy of Vietnam. At the June 23, 2005, Senate Armed Services Committee hearing on the war in Iraq, General John Abizaid, Commander of U.S. Central Command, which includes the Middle East, asked what he thought of Vice President Cheney's most recent statement that the "insurgency in Iraq is in its last throes," answered, "I'm sure you'll forgive me from criticizing the Vice President."

A Pentagon official, speaking under conditions of anonymity, said, when questioned about the future of the volunteer army, "The bottom line, in my view, is we are going to need some sort of national service, a draft, to get the people we need. I don't see what else we can do."

The military will need the draft, not only to send home the National Guard and Reserve units, but to keep the regular units from having to go back a third and fourth time. This time, though, America will have caught on, and for better and worse, it will be a draft without privilege, without concocted defer-ments for the wealthy and the connected, where everyone who is eligible, will go.

When America stopped drafting its citizens in 1973, it did not abolish the Selective Service System's machinery that had scooped up 15 million young men to fight World War II and 20,000 a month to fight in Vietnam. That same Selective Service System remains in place. It simply has to be turned on.

And that is the quandary in which this government has placed both itself, the military and the country. To decrease the risks to troops already in Iraq and Afghanistan, more troops will have to be put at risk.

But to send in more troops will be to increase the overall numbers of those either threatened or at peril. It is at best a Hobson's choice. And one that should never have even been considered. But there is always a danger in ignoring the past. The French could have told President Johnson, MacNamara, and McBundy about fighting in Vietnam and the British could have told Bush, Cheney, and Rumsfeld about fighting in Iraq.

Ours is not the first occupation of Iraq by a modern high-tech army determined to bring Western Civilization and Democracy to one of the most dangerous neighborhoods in world. The British tried to do just that for forty years after World War I. Over those decades, the British government committed tens of thousands of troops to the deserts of Iraq, squandered the wealth of their nation, and in the end had to leave.

In 1936, twenty years into the British occupation, a Royal Air Force intelligence officer, Alan MacDonald, in a memoir describing his service in Iraq's predominantly Shiite south, wrote, "Here in Iraq, we cannot breathe the words, we cannot accept the horrid fact, that we are unpopular, positively disliked, even hated. Old acceptances of Empire, color prejudices, an overweening complacency in our own abilities. Is one surprised that such self-satisfaction evokes resentment and anger?"

In 1947, with Iraq drifting toward chaos, Kermit Roosevelt, a grandson of Theodore Roosevelt and at the time CIA station chief in Cairo, wrote, as part of a position paper, after a visit to Baghdad, "The British have the politicians, but that is not much—they are a sorry, shaky lot, hardly worth owning. If it weren't for British protection, which allowed them to build up their own secret police and army, much of the government would be murdered in two hours."

There are those on the ground today in Baghdad, Mosul, or along the Iraq borders with Syria and Iran who have begun to consider that our efforts might not end much differently...

Blinded

There is a Talmudic admonition that in order to truly understand something, indeed to know anything, you must first be able to name it. But in modern times, it is not names, but numbers that matter. It is by numbers that we are taught to know things. It is by numbers that we are swayed, that we decide what is good and what is bad, what is successful and what is not, what should be supported and what abandoned. It was once understood that while numbers could give the price of things, they could not give us the value. Now they tell everything. They are certainly how we have come to know our wars.

Despite the 450,000 Americans wounded in Vietnam, it was the number of deaths that turned America against the war. A kind of urban legend developed during the Vietnam War that continued on after the war and is perpetuated today by those who continue to support our involvement in that war. It was proposed even as our armies began to fail that it was the reporting of bad news that lost us Vietnam. Those who had written critically of that war are chastised even today for focusing on only the bad news from the battlefield, while ignoring the "clear" successes. The view held then, as now, that it was the *New York Times* and *Washington Post,* along with the AP and UPI, that poisoned America and turned the nation against "staying the course." Yet anyone who was there knows that it wasn't the truth that led to our failure in Vietnam—it was the numbers.

If there had never been a single reporter in Vietnam; if a single article had never been written about how poorly the war was going; even if no one had ever mentioned the clear and deepening flaws in our strategy and tactics, the shortcomings and eventual failings of the South Vietnam Army, the growing antagonism and deepening deterioration of morale among U.S. troops, along with our leaders continuing belief that we could achieve victory at a smaller cost than our enemy was prepared to make us pay, the war would have ended in much the same way.

The ever-increasing number of body bags coming home each month would have become harder and harder to ignore. The public would have eventually demanded some kind of accounting that no amount of spin about the "light at the end of the tunnel," "building democracy," or "the domino theory" could explain away. In the end no matter what was said or whatever the explanations for the continuing deaths, we would have taken our helicopters and fighter bombers, our tanks and our troops, and—along with our dead—gone home.

The point is that death is easy to understand. It is not some abstract concept or some vague fact easy to manipulate or ignore. It is real and immediate. No confusion, no excuses. Everyone knows what death means.

A government might refuse to allow photographs of returning caskets, might pull programs off TV that present the reading of the names of those already killed, or attack anyone who refuses to repeat all the happy talk of a war on course. But it doesn't work. Dying is not easy to manipulate. With death you can't pretend.

The wounded are another matter. Those numbers can still be spun or ignored, the consequences discounted or put off into the future. But in this war that is a big mistake. Wounds, too, can be forever. And like deaths on our other battlefields become the metaphor for all that is happening. Ask any neurologist . . .

"There are degrees of blindness. Not in seeing, but of perception. For the most part when sight is lost, it is lost for good. What changes over time is the remembrance of light . . . "

"The insurgency is in its last throes."

"The physiology of vision has been well-established.

Photons of light enter the eye through the iris and are focused by the crystalline lens on the light sensitive cells of the retina. These cells, the rods and cones are activated by the photons of light to send electrical signals through the optic nerves to the visual cortex of the brain. It is there in the visual cortex that the electrical signals are organized by the cortical cells with input from the thalamus and memory parts of the brain into visual images."

"We will be welcomed as liberators." *Injury to any of these neurological pathways will lead to blindness. But with these pathway injuries there is also an ongoing and profound alteration in the brain's intrinsic intra-organization of sight."*

"The commanders on the ground do not need more troops."

"Much like a muscle that atrophies after its nerves are cut, the visual cortex of the brain gradually loses its ability to remember as that sense of vision itself begins to diminish."

"There will be a draw-down of military troops within three months of the fall of Baghdad."

"Immediately following a traumatic eye injury, damage to the optic nerve or to the visual cortex, through a penetrating head wound, asphyxia or a TBI, the patient begins to lose that sense of light itself, that loss continuing to diminish over months and years, gradually and irrevocably evolving into a profound psychological sense of impenetrable darkness—a growing blackness that eventually leaves the patient devoid of any sense of light, as first the remembrance of lightness and then the very sense of brightness itself begins to fail. . . . "

We Are All Wounded

In a very real way, this book was begun within six weeks of the start of the war. There was something wrong from the very beginning, a sense on the part of those of us who had been in the military, that despite the pronouncements of success, things didn't seem to be going well. The day that President Bush landed on the aircraft carrier USS *Abraham Lincoln*, under the banner "Mission Accomplished," two soldiers were killed and a dozen troopers wounded near Faluga.

Those casualties were not mentioned that day in the press nor by the administration. And none of those embedded reporters or anyone in the Pentagon remarked that during the race up to Baghdad, the largest number of U.S. casualties were in support units being ambushed along the Army's increasingly extended supply lines. There was a kind of opaqueness in the air, a gap between what appeared to be happening and what we were being told.

Concerned and a bit worried, I simply started talking to those I knew in the Army and Marines, those on active duty or in the National Guard or Reserves serving in Iraq or Afghanistan. It seemed to me that if you wanted to know what was happening that you had to talk to those involved—the ones on the ground, to those taking the risks and doing the fighting.

It did not take long to figure out that the casualties of this war were quickly outpacing the deaths and that whatever the administration or the Pentagon might say about the dangers of fighting in Iraq or Afghanistan, the real risk to our troops, at times ten and fifteen to one, was not in being killed but in being wounded.

At about the same time that the Pentagon put photographs of caskets coming home off limits, I noticed a new word creeping into the lexicon of military medicine . . . Polytrauma. The medics and the military physicians clearly knew what was happening and felt the need to change the vocabulary to meet the realities of the battlefield, even as the country was being kept in the dark.

The surviving wounded are of a nature completely different from the wounded in any of our other wars. This is a particularly brutal and violent fight and that ferocity needed a new more violent name. "Polytrauma," in its straightforwardness and simplicity, is precisely that word. Today's survivors are more damaged—and damaged in more and different ways than anyone had expected—nor had ever seen before.

This newest type of casualty coming out of this our newest war involves severe and devastating multiple traumas: severe head injuries, vision and hearing loss, nerve damage, bone fractures, contaminated wounds, severed limbs, transected spinal cords along with emotional and behavioral problems. And the numbers of patients with these multiple awful wounds increase every month of the war.

It has only been recently that the once embedded reporters have begun to report on what was so clear within weeks, if not months, of our going to war...that the "Shock and Awe" was not the Tomahawk Missile or the GPS-guided five-hundred-pound bomb, but the roadside bomb and the suicide bomber. A few 105mm shells linked together and surrounded by fifty pounds of high explosives can kill or injure everyone inside a Humvee or turn over a twenty-four-ton armored personnel carrier.

Somewhere along the line, I did try to find out the exact numbers of amputees coming out of Iraq and was told by an officer at Walter Reed, nervously though as if it were a joke, that he would like to tell me, but that the number was a military secret. The military physicians and nurses at the Combat Surgical Hospitals in Iraq and the Evacuation Hospitals in Europe are decidedly less discreet and definitely less cautious. "These are horrific, awful wounds. We may be keeping these patients alive, but they will never be the same." And it is not an exaggeration to say that it happens every day in twos and threes and sometimes the half dozens.

After almost three years, the media are finally catching up or at least catching on. In January of 2006, the *New York Times* reported ". . . with better battlefield care and protective gear, the military is saving more wounded; yet, the insurgent's heavy reliance on car bombs and buried explosives means survivors are more damaged then ever before."

It baffles me that families are still willing to send their sons and daughters into a war without any front lines, where each day, troops mount up to patrol the most dangerous roads in the world, hoping as they start out that they will come back that night alive and intact.

But if you want to know the price we've paid for looking for weapons of mass destruction and trying to bring democracy to a land that has been in turmoil for some 3,000 years, then all you have to do is wonder the next time you see a young man or woman in a wheelchair or without an arm or legs "how did this happen". . . or right now you can get on the Internet and chat with the young wife of a Marine from the First Marine Division or a trooper from the Third Armored Cavalry and ask if her husband on some orthopedic or neurosurgery ward can manage to eat by himself or if he is finally able to say a few words . . . You listen to her and you understand why we are all wounded . . .

REFERENCES AND
RECOMMENDED READINGS

Foreword

Hall, Donald. "Distressed Haiku." *The Painted Bed: Poems*. New York: Houghton Mifflin, 2002.

All the Pauls

Foss, Christopher F. *The Encyclopedia of Tanks and Armored Fighting Vehicles*. Los Angeles: Thunder Bay Press, 2002.

Thompson, Peter. *The Real Insider's Guide to Military Basic Training*. Honesdale, PA: Universal, 2003.

Wright, Evan. *Generation Kill: Devil Dogs, Iceman, Captain America and the New Face of American War*. New York: Penguin, 2004.

Medics

Bowden, Mark. *Black Hawk Down: A Story of Modern War*. New York: Penguin, 2000.

Cramer, Eric. "Technology Boosting Survival Rate in Iraq." *Army News Service*. October 31, 2003.

De Tocqueville, Alexis. *Democracy in America*. New York: Signet Classic, 2001.

Gawande, Atul. "Casualties of War—Military Care for the Wounded from Iraq and Afghanistan." *New England Journal of Medicine*. December 9, 2004.

Grossman, John. "Emergency! Emergency Trauma Care" *Health*. July, 1989.

"How the Marine Corps Trains Leaders." *Fortune*. September 2005.

Knickmeyer, Ellen. "Under U.S. Design, Iraq's New Army Looks a Good Deal Like the Old One." *Washington Post*. November 21, 2005.

McCarthy, Michael. "U.S. Military Revamps Combat Medic Training and Care." *The Lancet.* vol. 361. February 8, 2003.

"The Mobile Army Surgical Hospital (MASH): A Military and Surgical Legacy." *Journal of the National Medical Association.* vol. 97, no. 5. May, 2005.

Numbers

Adams, Chris and Alison Young. "Discharged and Dishonored: Shortchanging America's Veterans." *Knight Ridder Newspapers.* March 6, 2005.

"Artificial Limbs, Real Help." *Minneapolis Star Tribune.* March 26, 2005.

Benjamin, Mark. "17,000 GIs Not Listed as Casualties." *United Press International.* September 16, 2004.

"The Invisible Wounded." *Salon.* March 8, 2005.

Dao, James. "Death Visits a Marine Unit, Once Called Lucky." *New York Times.* August 7, 2005.

"DoD Opens Amputee Care Center in Texas." *Orthotics and Prosthetics Business News.* March 2005.

Dunham, Will. "Another Iraq War Legacy: Badly Wounded U.S. Troops." *Reuters.* October 23, 2005.

Dwyer, Johnny. "The Wounded." *New York Times Magazine.* March 27, 2005.

Edsall, Thomas B. "V A Faces 2.6 Billion Shortfall in Medical Care." *Washington Post.* June 29, 2005.

Fernandez, Kim. "Paving the Way." *O + P Almanac.* March, 2005.

"FY 2006 Budget Submission Summary Volume." Office of Budget, Department of Veterans Affairs.

Galloway, Joseph. "Army is Broken and in Need of Repair." *Knight Ridder Newspapers.* October 12, 2005.

Galloway, Joseph. "How to Ruin a Great Army in a Short Time." *Knight Ridder Newspapers.* September 28, 2003.

Galloway, Joseph. "Now's the Time for a Clear Eyed Look at Where We Are in Iraq." *Knight Ridder Newspapers.* June 1, 2005.

"Farewell to David Salie, the Best of the Best." *Knight Ridder Newspapers.* February 16, 2005.

"VA Should Expedite the Implementation of Recommendations

Needed to Improve Post-Traumatic Stress Disorder Services." GAO Report. February, 2005.

Goodman, Amy. "Veterans Return From Iraq Disabled and Homeless" *Democracy Now.* December 13, 2004.

Herbert, Bob. "My Pain Deep Inside." *New York Times.* August 8, 2005.

"Iraq War Amputees Get New Limbs, New Life." *Associated Press.* March 8, 2005.

Little, Bernard S. "Walter Reed Breaks Ground for Amputee Training Center." *Army News Service.* November 22, 2004.

Metz, Rachel. "Embracing the Artificial Limb." *Wired News.* February 18, 2005.

Moss, Michael. "Bloodied Marines Sound Off About Want of Armor and Men." *New York Times.* April 25, 2005.

Opel, Richard A. "Magnet for Iraq Insurgents is a Crucial Test of New U.S. Strategy." *New York Times.* June 1, 2005.

Pace, Eric. "General Westmoreland, Who Led U.S. in Vietnam, Dies." *New York Times.* July 19, 2005.

Starks, Tim. "Veterans' Groups Make Case for Health Care Dollars as Spending Bill Heads to Markup." *Congressional Quarterly Today.* May 17, 2005.

Summers, Harry G. *On Strategy: A Critical Analysis of the Vietnam War.* New York: Dell, 1982.

Vick, Karl. "The Lasting Wounds of War; Roadside Bombs Have Devastated Troops and Doctors Who Treat Them." *The Washington Post.* April 27, 2004.

Things

"A Science Fiction Army." Editorial. *New England Journal of Medicine.* March 31, 2005.

"Defending America." Editorial. *New York Times.* July 10, 2005.

Galloway, Joseph. "Learning Lesson of Vietnam All Over Again." *Knight Ridder Newspapers.* July 6, 2005.

Graham, Bradley. "Every Body Counts." *Washington Post.* October 24, 2003.

Herbert, Bob. "Dangerous Incompetence." *New York Times.* June 30, 2005.

Jaffe, Greg. "Rumsfeld Pushes Major Revamping of U.S. Military." *Wall Street Journal.* March 11, 2005.

Kitfield, James. *Prodigal Soldiers: How the Generation of Officers Born of Vietnam Revolutionized the American Style of War.* New York: Simon and Schuster, 1995.

Macgregor, Douglas A. *Breaking the Phalanx.* New York: Praeger, 1997.

Macgregor, Douglas A. *Transformation Under Fire: Revolutionizing How America Fights.* New York: Praeger, 2003.

Rich, Frank. "Forget Armor. All You Need is Love." *New York Times.* January 30, 2005.

Summers, Harry G. *On Strategy: A Critical Analysis of the Vietnam War.* New York: Dell, 1982.

"Support Our Troops." Editorial. *New York Times.* May 1, 2005.

Tyson, Ann Scott. "Horror Glimpsed from the Inside of a Humvee in Iraq." *Washington Post.* April 21, 2005.

Final Diagnosis

Arun, Neil. "Shaped Bombs Magnify Iraq Attacks." *BBC News.* October 10, 2005.

Castaneda, Antonia. "Last Marine in Squad Mourns 11 Friends Killed in Bombing." *Associated Press.* April 10, 2005.

"The Conflict Iraq: Protective Armor." *New York Times.* April 25, 2005.

DePalma Ralph G. "Blast Injuries." *New England Journal of Medicine.* vol. 352, no. 13. March 31, 2005.

Galloway, Joseph "Now's the Time for a Clear-Eyed Look at Where We are in Iraq." *Knight Ridder Newspapers.* June 1, 2005.

Jontz, Sandra. "Head Injuries Push Improvements in Gear." *Stars and Stripes.* January 30, 2004.

Mishra, Raja. "Amputation Rate for US Troops Twice that of Past Wars." *Boston Globe.* December 9, 2004.

"More Americans Dying from Roadside Bombs in Iraq." www.realcities.com. July 10, 2005.

Moss, Michael. "Man Missteps Tied to Dealy in Armor for Troops in Iraq." *New York Times.* March 7, 2005.

Nusbaumer, Steward. "The Cost of War at Walter Reed." *Intervention Magazine.* October 20, 2005.

Okie, Susan. "Traumatic Brain Injury in the War Zone." *New England Journal of Medicine*. vol. 352, no. 20. May 19, 2005.

Ricks, Thomas E. "Where Does Iraq Stand Among U.S. Wars?" *Washington Post*. May 31, 2004.

Satz, P., D. L. Fourney and K. Zaucha, et al. "Depression, Cognition, and Functional Correlates of Recovery Outcome After Traumatic Brain Injury." *The Journal of Brain Injury*. vol. 12:537:553. 1998.

Wagner, Chuck. "Brain Injuries High Among Iraq Casualties." *Army News Service*. November 24, 2003.

Wessely, Simon. "Victimhood and Resilience." *New England Journal of Medicine*. vol. 353, no. 6. August 11, 2005.

Shell Shock

Amburn, Brad. "Brain Injuries Lead to War Injuries." *United Press International*. July 23, 2004.

"Americans as Survivors." *New England Journal of Medicine*. vol. 352, no. 22. June 2, 2005.

"Analysis of V A Health Care." *VA Office of Public Health and Environmental Hazards*. March 15, 2005.

Bowser, Betty Ann. "Coping with War." *PBS "The NewsHour with Jim Lehrer."* November 9, 2004.

Brunswick, Mark. "Suddenly Soldiers." *Minneapolis Star Tribune*. September 18, 2005.

Figley, Charles R. *Mapping Trauma in Its Wake*. New York: Brunner-Routledge. 2005.

Friedman, Matthew. "Post-Traumatic Stress Disorder in the Military Veteran." *Psychiatric Clinics of North America*. vol. 17, no. 2. June 1994.

"Veterans' Mental Health in the Wake of War." *New England Journal of Medicine*. March 31, 2005.

Hoge, Charles W. et al. "Combat Duty in Iraq and Afghanistan, Mental Health Problems, and Barriers to Care." *New England Journal of Medicine*. vol. 351, no. 1. July 1, 2004.

"Iraq Veterans May Create Strain on Rural Mental Health." www.kc.frb.org. July 5, 2005.

"The Irritable Heart of Solders and the Origins of Anglo-American Cardiology." *New England Journal of Medicine*. vol. 348, no. 16. April 17, 2003.

Jaffe, Greg. "I Am Not the Same Person: For Nate Self, Battlefield Hero, Trauma Takes Toll." *Wall Street Journal*. October 6, 2005.

Kardiner, Abram. *War Stress and Neurotic Illness*. New York: Hoeber, 1947.

Lumpkin, John J. "Iraq Affecting Mental Health of Troops." *Associated Press*. July 29, 2005.

Matsakis, Aphrodite. *Vietnam Wives: Facing the Challenge of Life with Veterans Suffering Post-Traumatic Stress*. San Francisco: Sidran Press, 1996.

Offley, Ed. "Norman Schwarzkopf Braved Minefields in his Personal and Military Life."*Seattle Post Intelligencer*. October 6, 1992.

Sand, Paul. "More Vets Waiting for Care." *Minneapolis Star Tribune*. June 6, 2005.

Shakespeare, William. *Julius Caesar*. Act II, Scene I.

Shane, Scott. "A Deluge of Troubled Soldiers is in the Offing, Experts Predict." *New York Times*. December 16, 2004.

Walsh, Edward. "Vietnam Groups Critical of Bush's VA Budget." *Washington Post*. March 3, 2004.

Woolsey, Charles F. *The Irritable Heart of Soldiers*. New York: Ashgate Publishers Ltd., 2002.

Oaths

Bloche, M. Gregg. "When Doctors Go to War." *New England Journal of Medicine*. vol. 352, no. 1. January 6, 2005.

Herbert, Bob. "Who We Are." *New York Times*. August 1, 2005.

Lewis, Neil A. "Military Doctors Aided Guantanamo Interrogators." *New York Times*. June 24, 2005.

Military Tribunal at Guantanamo Bay. *The Lancet*. vol. 362. August 16, 2003.

"Reprimand Sought, Rejected for Guantanamo Commander." *Minneapolis Star Tribune*. July 13, 2005.

A Matter of Class

Brunswick, Mark. "It Would Be Minnesota Guards' Largest Mobilization Since WWII." *Minneapolis Star Tribune*. October 10, 2005.

Bunting, Josiah. "Class Warfare." *The American Scholar*. Winter 2005.

Burns, John. "Choose: More Troops in Iraq Will (Help)(Hurt)." *New York Times*. June 19, 2005.

Cave, Damien. "For Army Recruiters, a Hard Toll from a Hard Sell." *New York Times*. March 27, 2005.

"Pentagon Proposes Rise in Age Limit for Recruits." *New York Times*. July 22, 2005.

Cloud, David. "Part Time Forces on Active Duty Decline Steeply." *New York Times*. July 11, 2005.

Galloway, Joseph. "Army Lowers Standards and Increases Bonuses, But Still Falling Short of Recruiting Goal." *Knight Ridder Newspapers*. June 14, 2005.

Galloway, Joseph. "Army Moves to Recruit More High School Dropouts." *Knight Ridder Newspapers*. October 4, 2005.

Herbert, Bob. "An Army Ready to Snap." *New York Times*. November 10, 2005.

"The Army's Hard Sell." *New York Times*. June 17, 2005.

Krugman, Paul. "Too Few, Yet Too Many." *New York Times*. May 30, 2005.

Matheson, Kathy. "Seven PA Guardsmen Killed in Less Than Four Days." *Associated Press*. August 11, 2005.

Meyer, Karl E. "Forty Years in the Sand." *Harper's*. June 2005.

"Parents' Opposition Biggest Obstacle Potential Recruits Face." *Minneapolis Star Tribune*. July 14, 2005.

Rich, Frank. "The Vietnamization of Bush's Vacation." *New York Times*. August 28, 2005.

Truscott, Lucian K. "The Not-So-Long-Gray Line." *New York Times*. June 28, 2005.

Blinded

Carter, Graydon. "The Forgotten War." *Vanity Fair*. June 20, 2005.

Herbert, Bob. "Dangerous Incompetence." *New York Times*. June 30, 2005.

Thomas, Evan. "War of Nerves." *Newsweek*. July 4, 2005.

We Are All Wounded

Grady, Denise. "The Wounded—Surviving Multiple Injuries." *New York Times*. January 22, 2006.